Liqui...

PENGUIN BOOKS

TEACH LIKE YOUR HAIR'S ON FIRE

Rafe Esquith has taught at Hobart Elementary School for twenty-four years. He is the only teacher in history to receive the National Medal of Arts. He has also been made a Member of the British Empire by Queen Elizabeth. His many other honors include the American Teacher Award, *Parents* magazine's As You Grow Award, Oprah Winfrey's Use Your Life Award, and the Compassion in Action Award from the Dalai Lama. He is the author of three books, including *Lighting Their Fires,* and lives in Los Angeles with his wife, Barbara Tong.

Visit www.hobartshakespeareans.org

TEACH LIKE YOUR HAIR'S ON FIRE

The Methods and Madness
Inside Room 56

RAFE ESQUITH

PENGUIN BOOKS

PENGUIN BOOKS
Published by the Penguin Group
Penguin Group (USA) Inc., 375 Hudson Street, New York, New York 10014, U.S.A. •
Penguin Group (Canada), 90 Eglinton Avenue East, Suite 700, Toronto,
Ontario, Canada M4P 2Y3 (a division of Pearson Penguin Canada Inc.) • Penguin Books Ltd, 80
Strand, London WC2R 0RL, England • Penguin Ireland, 25 St. Stephen's Green, Dublin 2, Ireland
(a division of Penguin Books Ltd) • Penguin Group (Australia), 250 Camberwell Road, Camberwell,
Victoria 3124, Australia (a division of Pearson Australia Group Pty Ltd) • Penguin Books India Pvt Ltd,
11 Community Centre, Panchsheel Park, New Delhi – 110 017, India • Penguin Group (NZ),
67 Apollo Drive, Rosedale, North Shore 0632, New Zealand (a division of Pearson New Zealand Ltd)
• Penguin Books (South Africa) (Pty) Ltd, 24 Sturdee Avenue,
Rosebank, Johannesburg 2196, South Africa

Penguin Books Ltd, Registered Offices: 80 Strand, London WC2R 0RL, England

First published in the United States of America by Viking Penguin,
a member of Penguin Group (USA) Inc. 2007
Published in Penguin Books 2007

3 5 7 9 10 8 6 4

The photographs on pages 30, 67, 88, 94, 102, 111, 114, 118, 134, 136, 192,
and 205 are by Heather Harris and Kurt Ingham. Used by permission.
The illustration on page 70 is Copyright 1984 by Marcy Cook. Used by permission.
The illustration on page 155 is by Andy Hahn.

AUTHOR'S NOTE: Although this book is based on true events, the students and teachers
described are either composites of individuals I have observed over twenty-five years of teaching
or their names and characteristics have been changed. Any attempt by an individual to identify
him or herself would be a mistake. The only individual flaws in this book are my own.

ISBN 978-0-670-03815-2 (hc.)
ISBN 978-0-14-311286-0 (pbk.)
CIP data available

Printed in the United States of America

For the Hobart Shakespeareans,
who have been my best teachers . . .

and for Barbara

Contents

Prologue: Fire in the Classroom   *ix*

PART ONE: THERE'S NO PLACE LIKE HOME

ONE: Gimme Some Truth   3

TWO: Searching for Level VI   13

PART TWO: THE METHOD

THREE: Reading for Life   29

FOUR: Writing   45

FIVE: Add It Up   62

SIX: We Won't Get Fooled Again   73

SEVEN: What a Wonderful World   85

EIGHT: Rocket Man   96

NINE: Art Lover   106

TEN: Put Me In, Coach   123

ELEVEN: Taxman   133

PART THREE: THE MADNESS

TWELVE: Think for Yourself   145

THIRTEEN: Celluloid Heroes   159

FOURTEEN: Goin' Mobile   172

FIFTEEN: It's Only Rock 'n' Roll (but I Like It)   190

SIXTEEN: Do They Know It's Christmas?   201

SEVENTEEN: Will Power   208

EPILOGUE: Rest in Peace   224

Acknowledgments   *229*

Appendixes   *231*

Fire in the Classroom

It is a strange feeling to write this book. I am painfully aware that I am not superhuman. I do the same job as thousands of other dedicated teachers who try to make a difference. Like all *real* teachers, I fail constantly. I don't get enough sleep. I lie awake in the early-morning hours, agonizing over a kid I was unable to reach. Being a teacher can be painful.

For almost a quarter of a century, I have spent the majority of my time in a tiny, leaky classroom in central Los Angeles. Because of a little talent and a lot of luck, I have been fortunate to receive some recognition for my work. Not a day goes by when I do not feel overwhelmed by the attention.

I doubt that any book can truly capture the Hobart Shakespeareans. However, it is certainly possible to share some of the things I've learned over the years that have helped me grow as a teacher, parent, and person. For almost twelve hours a day, six days a week, forty-eight weeks a year, my fifth-graders and I are crowded into our woefully insufficient space, immersed in a world of Shakespeare, algebra, and rock 'n' roll. For the rest of the year, the kids and I are on the road. While my wife believes me to be eccentric, good friends of mine have not been so gentle, going as far as to label me quixotic at best and certifiable at worst.

I don't claim to have all the answers; at times it doesn't feel as if I'm reaching as many students as I succeed with. I'm here only to share some of the ideas I have found useful. Some of them are just plain common sense, and others touch on insanity. But there is a method to this madness. It is my hope that some parents and teachers out there will agree with me that our culture is a disaster. In a world that considers athletes and pop stars more important than research scientists and firefighters, it has become practically impossible to develop kind and brilliant individuals. And yet we've created a different world in Room 56. It's a world where character matters, hard work is respected, humility is valued, and support for one another is unconditional. Perhaps when parents and teachers see this, and realize that my students and I are nothing special, they will get a few ideas and take heart.

I am sad when I see so many good teachers and parents surrender to forces that sap their potential excellence. The demons are everywhere. Those who care deeply often feel outgunned by apathetic or incompetent administrators and politicians. Expectations for children are often ridiculously low. Racism, poverty, and ignorance often reign supreme on campus. Add to this mix ungrateful students, and even mean-spirited people in the teaching profession itself, and the hardiest of souls can be crushed. Each defeat usually means that a child's true potential will not be developed.

I was fortunate to have a ridiculous moment in the classroom that literally lit my way out of the darkness. Years ago, feeling tired and frustrated, I spent a few weeks searching my soul and did something I rarely do—I questioned whether teaching was worth it anymore. A combination of the aforementioned demons had beaten me down, and I was practically down for the count.

But for some reason, when I was guilty of feeling sorry for myself, I spent a day paying extra attention to a kid in class whom I liked very much. She was one of those kids who always seem to be the last one picked for the team, a quiet girl who appeared to have accepted the idea that she could never be special. I was determined to convince her that she was wrong.

I was teaching a chemistry lesson, and the students were excited about working with alcohol lamps. But the girl couldn't get her wick to burn. The rest of the class wanted to move on with their projects, but I told everyone to wait. I was not going to leave her behind, even after she told me to continue with the others and not worry about her.

Normally I do not interfere with science projects, because failure can be part of the learning process. Yet this was simply a matter of faulty equipment; it had nothing to do with the chemical principle we were exploring that morning. I needed to step in. The girl had tears in her eyes, and I felt ashamed of myself for ever having felt like giving up. Suddenly her sadness was all that mattered.

Athletes often refer to getting "into the zone" when they forget about the crowd and the pressure and see only the ball. It can happen in other fields too. For that one moment, the only thing that mattered to me was that this girl should have a successful experiment. She was going to go home that day with a smile on her face. I bent closely over the wick of her alcohol lamp. For some reason the wick was not as long as it should have been—I could barely see it. I leaned as close as I could, and with a long kitchen match tried to reach it. I was so close to the match that I could feel the flame as I tried to ignite the lamp. I was determined to get the lamp working. And it started working! The wick caught fire, and I looked up triumphantly to see the smile I expected on the girl's face.

Instead, she took one look at me and began screaming in fear. Other kids started yelling as well. I did not understand why they were all pointing at me, until I realized that while I was lighting the lamp, the flame had touched my hair; it was now smoldering and scaring the hell out of the children. Several of them ran to me and swiped at my head. Talk about a dream come true—they got to hit their teacher on the head and say they were trying to help him.

A few minutes later, all was well and the experiment proceeded. I felt (and looked) like an idiot. And yet for the first time in weeks, I felt great about being a teacher. I had been able to ignore the crap that all teachers on the front lines face. I had done everything I could to help someone. I didn't do it particularly well, but the effort was there. I thought to myself that if I could care so much about teaching that I didn't even realize my hair was burning, I was moving in the right direction. From that moment, I resolved to always teach like my hair was on fire.

There are so many charlatans in the world of education. They teach for a couple of years, come up with a few clever slogans, build their Web sites, and hit the lecture circuit. In this fast-food society, simple solutions to complex problems are embraced far too often. We can do better. I hope that people who read this book realize that true excellence takes sacrifice, mistakes, and enormous amounts of effort. After all, there are no shortcuts.

PART ONE

THERE'S NO PLACE LIKE HOME

—∿∿∿∿∿∿—

How Room 56 Creates a Safe Haven,
and Provides Children with
Shelter from the Storm

ONE

Gimme Some Truth

The parents want one of the teachers arrested. I have been summoned from my room by a mother who has known me for years. Some of the parents are demanding that the teacher be fired. I listen to their complaints and try to calm them down. I do the best I can to defend the teacher with whom they are furious, but it isn't easy.

Alex is a third-grader with a messy backpack. In fact, it's more than messy—it's a virtual nuclear holocaust of crumpled-up papers, folders, and candy. Here's an opportunity for his teacher to teach him something valuable. Instead, he began by yelling at Alex and dumping his backpack all over his desk in full view of his peers. Then he called on a student to go to his car and retrieve a camera. He took a picture of the mess and told Alex that he would hang it up during Back-to-School Night to show all the parents what a slob he was. Then the teacher added the final touch: He told Alex's classmates that for the rest of the day, when they had trash to discard, it should be thrown on Alex's desk instead of in the garbage can.

Now the boy's parents are in my room demanding that the authorities be called.

After enormous effort, I calm them down and beg them to let our principal handle the situation. The teacher must be given the chance to explain his actions, although it's clear that if his behavior was as cruel and humiliating as it sounds, no explanation can justify it.

Days later, after several meetings with the principal, the young teacher emerges from the office, face tear-stained and posture slumped with contrition. Yet he comes to me and bitterly defends himself. "But I'm right. *It worked . . . Alex's backpack is neater now.*" And I realize the real tragedy here is that the teacher has missed a terrific opportunity. He had a chance to help Alex learn the value of organization and become a better student. Instead, he forever marked himself as a cruel ogre to Alex and his classmates. It would take months to undo the harm of such a moment, and the teacher did not even comprehend the damage he had done.

The larger problem here is that many teachers are so desperate to keep their classrooms in order that they will do *anything* to maintain it. This is understandable—an "End justifies the means" mentality is at the heart of many explanations of how children are handled these days. Given some of the practically impossible situations confronting teachers today, it seems reasonable.

But let's be honest. It might be explicable. It might be effective. But it is not good teaching. We can do better.

I know this because I've been there. I've fallen into the same trap. The simple truth is that most classrooms today are managed by one thing and one thing only: fear.

The teacher is afraid: afraid of looking bad, of not being liked, of not being listened to, of losing control. The students are even more afraid: afraid of being scolded and humiliated, of looking foolish in front of peers, of getting bad grades, of facing their parents' wrath. John Lennon got it right in "Working Class Hero" when he sang of being "tortured and scared . . . for twenty-odd years."

This is the issue that overshadows all others in the world of education. It is the matter of classroom management.

If your class is not in order, nothing good will follow. There will be no learning. The kids will not read, write, or calculate better. Children will not improve their critical thinking. Character cannot be built. Good citizenship will not be fostered.

There is more than one way to run a successful classroom—from using the philosophy of Thoreau to the philosophy of Mussolini. Over the last twenty-five years, I've tried practically everything to deal with the often maddening behavior of children in a school environment that accepts graffiti-covered walls and urine-soaked bathroom floors as normal.

Visitors to Room 56 never come away most impressed with the academic ability of the children, the style in which I present lessons, or the cleverness of the wall decorations. They come away shaking their heads over something else: the culture of the classroom. It's calm. It is incredibly civil. It's an oasis. But something is missing. Ironically, Room 56 is a special place not because of what it has, but because of what it is missing: fear.

In my early years, I actually planned to frighten the kids the first day of school. I wanted to make sure they knew I was boss. Some of my colleagues did the same, and we shared our supposed successes in getting the kids in order. Other classes were out of control, and we foolishly congratulated one another on our quiet classrooms, orderly children, and smooth-running days.

Then one day, many years ago, I watched a fantastic video featuring a first-rate special education teacher who told a story about his son and the Boston Red Sox. He had inherited a priceless baseball signed by all the players of the legendary 1967 Sox. When his young son asked to play catch with him, of course he warned the boy that they could never use that ball. Upon being asked why, the teacher realized that Carl Yastrzemski, Jim Lonborg, and the rest of the 1967 Sox meant nothing to his son. Instead of taking the time to explain, however, he simply told the boy they could not use the ball "because it had writing all over it."

A few days later, the boy once again asked his father to play catch. When his father reminded him that they could not use the ball with the writing, his little boy informed him that he had solved the problem: He had licked off all the writing!

Of course the father was ready to kill his own son. On second thought, however, he realized his boy had done nothing wrong. And from that day forward, the teacher carried the unsigned baseball with him everywhere he went. It reminded him that, when teaching or parenting, you must always try to see things from the child's point of view and never use fear as a shortcut for education.

Painful though it was, I had to admit that many children in my class were behaving the way they were because they were afraid. Oh, lots of kids liked the class and quite a few learned all sorts of wonderful lessons. But I wanted more. We spend so much time trying to raise reading and math scores. We push our kids to run faster and jump higher. Shouldn't we also try to help them become better human beings? In fact, all these years later, I've recognized that by improving the culture of my classroom, the ordinary challenges are navigated far more easily. It's not easy to create a classroom without fear. It can take years. But it's worth it. Here are four things I do to ensure the class remains a place of academic excellence without resorting to fear to keep the kids in line.

Replace Fear with Trust

On the first day of school, within the first two minutes, I discuss this issue with the children. While most classrooms are based on fear, our classroom is based on trust. The children hear the words and like them, but they are only words. It is deeds that will help the children see that I not only talk the talk but walk the walk.

I use the following example with the students on their first day. Most of us have participated in the trust exercise in which one person falls back and is caught by a peer. Even if the catch is made a hundred times in a row, the trust is broken forever if the friend lets you fall the next time as a joke. Even if he swears he is sorry and will never let you fall again, you can never fall back without a seed of doubt. My students learn the first day that a broken trust is irreparable. Everything else can be fixed. Miss your homework assignment? Just tell me, accept the fact that you messed up, and we move on. Did you break something? It happens; we can take care of it. But break my trust and the rules change. Our relationship will be okay, but it will never, ever be what it once was. Of course kids do break trust, and they should be given an opportunity to earn it back. But it takes a long time. The kids are proud of the trust I give them, and they do not want to lose it. They rarely do, and I make sure on a daily basis that I deserve the trust I ask of them.

I answer all questions. It does not matter if I have been asked them before. It does not matter if I am tired. The kids must see that I passionately want them to understand, and it never bothers me when they don't. During an interview, a student named Alan once told a reporter, "Last year, I tried to ask my teacher a question. She became angry and said, 'We've been over this. You weren't listening!' But I *was* listening! I just didn't get it! Rafe will go over something five hundred times until I understand."

We parents and teachers get mad at our kids all the time, and often for good reason. Yet we should never become frustrated when a student doesn't understand something. Our positive and patient response to questions builds an immediate and lasting trust that transcends fear.

Children Depend on Us, So Be Dependable

Far too many times, an adult promises a child a reward for good behavior. This in itself is a problem, which will be discussed in the next chapter, but even more problematic is when the adult breaks his or her promise.

I know a well-respected teacher who once told her class, on the first day of school, that at the end of the year she would take them on a very exciting trip. Practically every day, students who were not behaving properly were threatened with the punishment of not going on the special trip. Many students even did extra work to make sure they would be included. During the last week of school, the teacher announced to the children that she was moving away and would not be able to take them after all. I wish she had stuck around long enough to hear the bitter comments of her students. This betrayal not only ruined anything good she had done with the kids that year, but soured many of them on school and adults in general. I can't blame them. A broken trust has to be avoided at all costs.

Parents and teachers have to come through. If I tell the kids we are beginning a special art project on Friday, I have to deliver, even if it means running out to a twenty-four-hour Home Depot at 4:00 A.M. to get extra wood and brushes. Being constantly dependable is the best way to build up trust. We do not need to lecture the children about how we came through on a promise; let them figure out that they can trust us. It's a cliché, but our actions truly do speak louder than our words.

A nice bonus here is that, if trust has been established, the kids are far more understanding on the rare occasion when a promised activity needs to be postponed.

Discipline Must Be Logical

You need to maintain order in your classroom. However, never forget this basic truth about discipline: Children do not mind a tough teacher, but they *despise* an unfair one. Punishments must fit the crimes, and too often they do not. Once the kids see you as unfair, you've lost them.

Over the years, children have related to me their pet peeves regarding unjust punishments and illogical consequences. It usually goes something like this: A child is acting up in class; the teacher decides the entire class will miss playing baseball that afternoon. The kids take it, but they hate it. Many are thinking, *Kenny robbed the bank—why am I going to jail?* Another classic example: John does not do his math homework; his punishment is to miss art during the afternoon, or sit on a bench at recess. There is no connection here.

In Room 56, I strive to make our activities so exciting that the worst punishment for misbehavior is to be banned from the activity during which the misbehavior occurred. If a child is misbehaving during a science experiment, I can simply say, "Jason, you are not using the science materials properly, so please stand outside the group. You can watch the experiment but you may not participate. You will have another chance tomorrow." If a child is a poor sport during a baseball game, he is asked to sit on the bench. It's logical, and I make sure that when a child plays correctly, he will be allowed back on the field.

A few years ago, my group of Hobart Shakespeareans—a group of young thespians comprised of students from different classrooms who work with me each day after school—was asked to give a performance at one of the most prestigious venues in Los Angeles. They would have to miss two hours of school for the performance. All but one of the students' teachers were thrilled their students were given the opportunity. The lone objector was the same teacher who never wants his children to join orchestra or chorus. You've met the type: He believes his children can learn only from him. In this case the students eventually prevailed—their parents demanded that the kids be allowed to perform—but upon returning to school they were forced to write the following sentence one hundred times a day for a week: "In the future I will make more responsible choices about my education." By the end of the week, the children's disgust with this teacher's illogical actions prevented them from hearing anything he had to say for the rest of the year (even when it was something worthwhile). He was not fair. Game over. Mission not accomplished.

You Are a Role Model

Never forget that the kids watch you constantly. They model themselves after you, and you have to be the person you want them to be. I want my students to be nice and to work hard. That means I had better be the nicest and hardest-working person they have ever met. Don't even think of trying to deceive your kids. They are much too sharp for that.

If you want your kids to trust you, it takes consistent caring and effort on your part. Some of my students laugh bitterly at a teacher they once had. They discuss her in the most unflattering of terms. She often comes to school late. She doesn't even realize it, but she's lost them. Why would the kids listen to her lessons when her constant tardiness tells them they are not that important to her? When she lectures them, they smile and nod their heads. Inside they are thinking, *Screw you, lady.*

This teacher talks on her cell phone constantly. Even when the kids are being taken somewhere, their fearless leader walks in front of them gabbing on the phone. Of course there are family emergencies and situations in which a teacher legitimately needs to take a call, but this woman is on the phone with her boyfriend. The same teacher thinks she is "secretly" shopping online while the kids do their science assignments. She believes the kids do not know what she is doing. She is very much mistaken.

There are thousands of role-modeling moments during a day of teaching, but a few of them are opportunities waiting to be seized. In my youth, I had days like the young teacher with the child's back-pack. My behavior was never that extreme, but I would become angry and frustrated. I was wrong to do this. I hadn't learned that if you become angry over little things, the big issues are never even addressed. As a role model, the students need us to be advocates, not tyrants. I played the dictator enough as a young teacher to understand the futility of the role.

But that's the beauty of the job: You can learn from your mistakes. You can get better. In the process you may even stumble upon precious moments that can allow your students to soar higher than they ever thought possible. I had such a moment just recently.

Lisa was a very nice little girl in my class who struggled with all her work. She was not the sharpest knife in the drawer, and she had a father who got angry when I wrote on her papers that I felt she could do better.

One day I was walking around the room collecting a homework assignment. The children were supposed to have finished a simple crossword puzzle about Chief Crazy Horse, but Lisa could not find hers. It was early in the year and she desperately wanted to do well. I watched as she furiously searched several folders in her desk. Knowing I was behind her, she continued her desperate hunt for the missing page.

Rafe: *Lisa?*

Lisa: *Rafe, give me just a second. I have it. I did it. Please—*

Rafe: (Gently) *Lisa?*

Lisa: *Pleeease, Rafe. I really did it* (still frantically looking).

Rafe: (Practically singing) *Leeeesa?*

Lisa: (Stops the futile quest and looks up) *Yes?*

Rafe: *I believe you.*

Lisa: (Silence—a quizzical stare)

Rafe: *I believe you.*

Lisa: *You do?*

Rafe: (Gently, with a smile) *Of course I do, Lisa. I believe you did the assignment. But you know what?*

Lisa: *What?*

Rafe: *I think we have a bigger problem here.*

Lisa: (Meekly, after a long pause) *I'm not organized?*

Rafe: *Exactly! You need to be better organized. That's exactly right. Now, how about picking two friends here whom you trust.*

Lisa: *Lucy and Joyce.*

Rafe: *Okay. Today after lunch, how about having your friends help you reorganize your folders? Would that be all right?*

Lisa: (Relieved) *Okay . . .*

These are the opportunities to seize upon. Of course you're frustrated, but you can take potentially bad moments and turn them into good ones. In the course of a few minutes, I went from Lisa's potential nemesis to her trusted teacher and friend. The class, watching my every move, saw me as a person who was reasonable. These are the moments when you build trust.

Lisa never missed a homework assignment for the rest of the year.

It's harder to follow this path. Hey, you can point a rifle at the kids and they will listen to you, but is that all you want? These days I know better. By creating a firm but friendly refuge, the kids have the opportunity to grow into confident, happy human beings. It's not easy, and not all the children will ever earn such faith. Some will betray your confidence. Yet if we ask great things of our children, we must show them we believe great things are possible. Make every effort to remove fear from your classroom. Be fair. Be reasonable. You will grow as a teacher, and your students will amaze both you and themselves as they flourish in the safe haven you have built.

Trust me.

Searching for Level VI

With experience, patience, and lessons learned from failure, you can create a classroom based on trust. The students know you to be fair. You're dependable. The kids know that with you around, they're safe and they are going to learn something. A classroom based on trust and devoid of fear is a fantastic place for kids to learn.

But a foundation of trust is not an end result. It is not even a middle ground; it is only a good first step. We've all seen this time and time again: Students do a terrific job with a fine teacher, but one day the teacher calls in sick or has to attend a meeting. A substitute takes over, and the classroom that had previously functioned so well turns into a scene from *Animal House*.

Sadly, I've actually encountered teachers who are proud of this. They think it shows what wonderful teachers they are—that they can control kids when others cannot. Recently, I heard a teacher brag, "My kids only watch films with me. They say it's not good if I'm not around." This is a teacher who has forgotten that we may lead the class, but the students determine if a class is outstanding or mediocre.

Over the years, I have tried many different ways to develop a classroom culture in which students behaved well for all the right reasons. This alone is a tall order. Given a school environment in which kids urinate all over the bathroom floor, write on desks, and quite frankly don't want to be in school at all, it is difficult to find a common language by which to develop morality.

And then I found it. Most teaching victories come as a result of years of difficult and painful labor—there are very few "educational eurekas," where the lightbulb blazes over your head and you know where to go. But one glorious evening it happened to me.

I had been planning lessons around my favorite book, *To Kill a Mockingbird,* and was reading a study guide that analyzed the novel's characters in relation to Lawrence Kohlberg's Six Levels of Moral Development. I just loved it. The Six Levels were simple, easy to understand, and, most important, perfectly applicable to teaching young people exactly what I wanted them to learn. I quickly incorporated the Six Levels into my class, and today they are the glue that holds it together. Trust is always the foundation, but the Six Levels are the building blocks that help my kids grow as both students and people. I even used the Six Levels in raising my own children, and I am extremely proud of how they turned out.

I teach my students the Six Levels on the first day of class. I do not expect the kids to actually apply them to their own behavior immediately. Unlike simplistic approaches that tell us, "If you follow these twenty-seven rules, you too can have a successful child," the Six Levels take a lifetime of effort. They are a beautiful road map, and I am constantly amazed at how well my students respond to them.

Level I. I Don't Want to Get in Trouble

Most students are trained from the minute they enter school to be Level I thinkers. Practically all of their behavior is based on the fact that they want to avoid trouble. "Quiet down!" they frantically tell one another. "The teacher's coming!" They do homework to stay out of trouble. They walk in a line to keep the teacher happy. They listen in class to stay in the good graces of their instructor. And we teachers and parents reinforce this constantly by promising them trouble if they don't toe the line. "Wait till your father gets home," indeed.

But is this good teaching? Level I thinking is based on fear. Eventually we want our children to behave well not because they fear punishment but because they believe it is right.

On the first day of class, the kids are quick to admit that they have spent most of their lives at Level I. Of course, some have moved on, yet all of the children admit that "not getting in trouble" is still a guiding force in their behavior. Think back to your own childhood. How many of us really finished homework assignments (particularly the mindless ones) because it was the right thing to do? More often than not, weren't we simply trying to stay out of trouble?

I remember vividly my first year of teaching. One day I had to attend a math training meeting, and my class fell apart when I was away. The next time I had to miss class, I wanted to be sure the kids wouldn't "make me look bad" again. I promised them with ferocious certainty that those who did not listen to the substitute or do their work would suffer dire consequences upon my return. It worked superficially, but the children had learned nothing except to fear my anger and power. It took time to realize that this strategy was not really effective. Like many veteran teachers, I am embarrassed to think about the foolishness of my early years.

Now, on the first day of class, I begin a partnership with the children. After I request their trust and pledge my own, I ask the children to leave Level I thinking behind them. They'll never get anywhere in life if their prime motivation is so misguided. And I certainly won't make the mistake of fueling Level I thinking ever again.

Level II. I Want a Reward

Eventually children begin to make decisions for reasons other than avoiding trouble. But teachers are especially guilty of enforcing what in our class is identified as Level II thinking. I guess too many of us read B. F. Skinner in college. We learned that if children are rewarded for good behavior, they are more likely to repeat behavior we deem acceptable. There is, of course, truth in this. Whether the reward is candy, toys, or more time for sports, a dangling carrot can be a powerful inducement for good behavior.

I have visited middle school classrooms in which teachers use Level II thinking to encourage their students to finish homework. One history teacher I met pits his classes against each other in a competition to see which of them can complete the most homework. The winning class gets a prize at the end of the year. Apparently this teacher has forgotten that a knowledge of history is supposed to be the prize. When I spoke to the class that did the most homework, I learned that they were terrific at completing assignments and turning them in, but their understanding of history was shockingly limited.

In my early years of teaching I foolishly bought into the reward syndrome because it "works." If I needed to miss class and was terrified that my kids would give the substitute a bad time, I knew how to handle the situation: I'd tell the children, "If I get a good report from your teacher, we'll have a pizza party on Friday." The next day I would return to find a nice note from the sub. This allowed me to trick myself into believing I had done a good job with my students. After all, it was certainly better than scaring them, and the kids "liked me" more. Okay, go easy on me. I was young and inexperienced.

Parents also need to be wary of encouraging Level II thinking. It's great to give a child allowance money for doing chores. That's how our capitalist system works—you are paid for doing your job. The danger, however, is giving children gifts or money for *behaving* the right way. We need to show our children that proper behavior is expected, not rewarded.

These payoffs are common in classrooms across the country. As someone who is on the front lines every day, I am well aware that getting kids to behave is one of the toughest jobs in the world. We're all working way too many hours, and if a homework chart with gold stars gets kids to do their work, that's good enough for many. But it is no longer good enough for me.

I think we can all do better.

Level III. I Want to Please Somebody

As they grow up, kids also learn to do things to please people: "Look, Mommy, is this good?" They do the same things with teachers, chiefly with the charismatic or popular ones. They sit up straight and behave the way we hope they'll behave. But they do it for all the wrong reasons.

Young teachers are especially susceptible to this phenomenon (and I speak from personal experience here). When kids want to please you, it gives your ego a jolt. It's nice to have students show you what you think of as respect, to have them jump when you say jump.

In one instance, when a teacher returned from a day of absence, something also sadly funny happened. The substitute left a note and the teacher was thrilled to learn that the class had been fine, but one student in particular, Robert, was fantastic. He helped run the class. He showed the substitute where everything was kept. He was an assistant teacher. But here comes the ironic part. The teacher was so proud of Robert that he offered his prize student a reward—perhaps it was extra points for a test or a piece of candy. Robert refused it. He didn't do it for a reward. He was thinking above this. He did it for the teacher. He was proud of himself. And the teacher was proud of *himself*, too, because he had a little guy worshipping him. They were both proud of themselves and felt good.

Of course it's nice that Robert did a good job, and it's sweet that he did it to please his teacher. This is far better than the situation in most classrooms. We can cue the music and maybe Lulu can sing "To Sir with Love." But we can still do better. This is a point on which I simultaneously tease and challenge my own students. Do you brush your teeth for me? Do you tie your shoes for me? Do you see how silly that sounds? And yet many children still spend their days trying to please their teachers.

The desire to come through for parents is an even greater pressure. Many children are so desperate to please their parents they will even pick their colleges and majors to keep their folks happy. These same kids grow into frustrated adults who hate their jobs and can't understand why they are so displeased with their lives.

Well, at least they were trying to please *someone*.

But I think we can do even better.

Level IV. I Follow the Rules

Level IV thinking is very popular these days. With so many young people behaving badly, most teachers are trained to lay down the law on the first day of class. After all, it is essential that kids know the rules. The better teachers take the time to explain the "why" of certain rules, and many creative teachers get their students involved in the creation of class standards. The theory is that kids who are involved in generating classroom rules will be more invested in following them. There is truth in this.

I've seen many classrooms where such rules are posted on the wall. There are charts hastily scribbled by a teacher with too much work to do and other charts that would impress the board of a Fortune 500 company. I've seen rules that make sense (no fighting) and rules that make no sense at all (no laughing). Well, to each his own. The fact that different classes have different standards can actually be good—it teaches students to adjust to new situations in new environments.

I have no problem with rules. Obviously, children need to learn about boundaries and behavioral expectations. I am certainly not an anarchist. And when I come back from my day at the staff development meeting, am I glad that Robert behaved himself with the substitute? I am thrilled. This already puts Robert on the right path to success and far in front of his more mediocre peers. It tells me that Robert knows the rules (not all children do), accepts them (even fewer do), and is willing to carry them out. If Robert and his class are Level IV thinkers, they're doing much better than most. One could argue that these good ends justify the means. But if we want our children to receive a meaningful education, do we really want Robert to do things because Rule 27 says he should?

I met a teacher who had an interesting way of teaching his kids to say "Thank you." One of his rules was that if the teacher gave you something—a calculator or a baseball or a candy bar—you had three seconds to acknowledge his kindness by saying "Thank you." If you didn't do this, the gift was immediately taken back.

And it worked. The kids said it constantly. The only problem was that they had no real appreciation for the gifts they received. They were merely following a rule. Also, the "lesson" did not carry over into other areas of the kids' lives. One night I took these same children to see a play, and they were no more or less gracious than other children in the theater. They did not thank the ushers who handed them programs or helped them find their seats, and they did not thank the people who served them drinks at intermission. Their class rule was just that—a way of behaving in one class with one teacher.

It's also worth considering how many outstanding people would need to be erased from the history books if they had never looked beyond Level IV thinking. I teach my students that while rules are necessary, many of our greatest heroes became heroes by *not* following the rules. We have a national holiday for Martin Luther King Jr., and this heroic American would have accomplished nothing had he been only a Level IV thinker. Gandhi didn't follow the rules, and neither did Rosa Parks. Courageous labor leaders broke rules to help their workers. Thank goodness that people like Thoreau, Malcolm X, and Cesar Chavez had the temerity to think beyond Level IV. Extraordinary people throughout history have done this, and if we want our children to reach such heights, they need to know the rules but see past a chart on the wall. There will be times when the chart is not there. More important, there will be times when the chart is wrong.

Level IV is a good place to be, but we must try to do even better.

Level V. I Am Considerate of Other People

Level V is rarefied air for both children *and* adults. If we can help kids achieve a state of empathy for the people around them, we've accomplished a lot.

Just imagine a world of Level V thinkers. We'd never again have to listen to the idiot on the bus barking into his cell phone. No one would cut us off when we're driving or in line for a movie. Noisy neighbors would never disturb our sleep in a hotel at 2:00 A.M. What a wonderful world it would be, indeed.

After many years of trying to get this idea across to my students, I finally found success by introducing them to Atticus Finch and *To*

Kill a Mockingbird. At one point in the novel, Atticus gives his daughter, Scout, a piece of advice that perfectly illustrates Level V thinking: "You never really understand a person until you consider things from his point of view . . . until you climb inside his skin and walk around in it." Many of my students took this advice to heart and before long the idea began to snowball. Soon almost all of my kids were becoming extremely considerate of others. With Atticus Finch leading the way, I learned that the old cliché is true. Kindness really is contagious.

During these years, I received extraordinary thank-you notes from my substitute teachers. They were amazed that my students were able to modulate their voices throughout the day. When one sub asked the class why they spoke in whispers, the kids told him they did not want to disturb the students in the next room. When the teacher remarked that he was hot, several youngsters offered him cold bottled water they knew was stored in our small refrigerator.

Hotel employees also remarked that my students were the kindest and best behaved they had ever seen. Announcements were made by grateful pilots on airplanes that the Hobart Shakespeareans were on board, and planeloads of people applauded their quiet demeanor and extraordinary manners. I was very happy and proud to be their teacher.

But . . . you guessed it: I still think we can do better. While few things make me happier than encountering a young person who has reached Level V, I want my students to reach even higher. For a teacher, there is no more difficult assignment. But the fact that it is difficult does not mean we should not try. It can happen, and when it does, the gratification I feel makes up for every heartache, headache, and small paycheck I have ever received because of the crazy world of education.

I know we can do better because I've seen it happen.

Level VI. I Have a Personal Code of Behavior and I Follow It (the Atticus Finch Level)

Level VI behavior is the most difficult to attain and just as difficult to teach. This is because a personal code of behavior resides within the soul of an individual. It also includes a healthy dose of humility. This combination makes it almost impossible to model; by definition, Level VI behavior cannot be taught by saying, "Look at what I'm doing. This is how you should behave." In a way, it is like a catch-22.

I teach my students about Level VI in several ways. Since I cannot discuss my own personal codes, I try to help the kids identify them in others. There are any number of outstanding books and films in which the Level VI individual exists. It's fun for parents and teachers to find this type of thinker—they're all over the place once you begin looking. Let me tell you about a few of my favorites.

Each year my fifth-graders read the outstanding novel *A Separate Peace* by John Knowles. The book's hero, Phineas, is an extraordinary athlete and a Level VI thinker. One day he's at the swimming pool and notices that the school record for a swimming event is not held by a member of his class. Although he has never trained as a swimmer, he tells his friend Gene that he thinks he can break the record. He limbers up briefly, mounts the starting block, and asks his friend to time him with a stopwatch. A minute later, Gene is shocked to see that Phineas has broken the record. But Gene is disappointed because no one else saw it to make the record "official." He plans to call the local paper and have Phineas redo his feat the following day in the presence of an official timekeeper and reporters. Phineas declines, and he also instructs Gene not to tell anyone about his accomplishment. He wanted to break the record and did. Gene is dumbfounded, but my students are not. They have a language to describe and understand Phineas's character.

Or take the case of Bernard, the boy who lives next to Willy Loman and his family in Arthur Miller's *Death of a Salesman*. Bernard is constantly pestering Willy's children about school and studying and is seen as a nerd. Later in the play, as Willy desperately tries to understand his failures and those of his own children, Bernard shows up but is in a hurry. He is a lawyer and has a case. As he rushes off, Bernard's father mentions that the case will be tried in front of the United States Supreme Court. When Willy marvels that Bernard didn't mention this astonishing fact, Bernard's father tells Willy, "He doesn't have to. He's doing it."

Through these examples I try my best to battle ESPN and MTV, where posturing, trash talk, and "I'm king of the world" is the norm. I try to quietly show children a different way.

I also use films that feature Level VI thinkers. One such character is Will Kane, the sheriff in *High Noon,* played brilliantly by Gary Cooper. Gunmen come to kill him, and everyone in town wants Kane to flee, for different reasons. Some want the gunmen to control the town so business will be better. The deputy wants Kane to leave because he wants his job. Kane's wife, a Quaker, wants him to run from the fight for religious reasons. But Kane has to stay. It's who he is. And even when he's been deserted by all, when his life is on the line, he remains true to his code. That's a tall order to ask of our children, but I ask it of them anyway.

For my money, the best example of a Level VI thinker on film is Morgan Freeman's character of Red in *The Shawshank Redemption.* I am well aware that most elementary-school children are not ready to watch this mature film, but Room 56 is a special place and we watch it after school each year. Red is in prison, serving a life sentence for murder. Every ten years or so he comes up for parole. He faces the parole board a number of times during the film, and each time he tells the board he is a changed man. His appeal is always rejected. But in one glorious scene, after spending most of his life in prison, Red finds his voice. He tells the parole board he doesn't even know what rehabilitated means, at least in their terms. When he is asked if he feels regret for what he has done, he says he does. But he says this *not because it's what they want to hear or because he is in prison,* but because *he sincerely feels regret.* He has grown into a man who knows himself and has reached Level VI. He does not base his actions on fear, or a desire to please someone, or even on rules. He has his own rules. And he is released from prison.

If you are skeptical about trying to get kids to this level of thinking, I don't blame you. Any teacher who is sincere and ambitious about what he does opens himself up to colossal failures and heartbreaking disappointments. A while back, two former students returned to my school. Only a few years earlier, they had been smiling in my classroom. They had participated in extracurricular activities and performed Shakespeare. I took them on trips to Washington, D.C., Mount Rushmore, the Grand Tetons, and Yellowstone National Park; I have a photo album full of pictures of these boys smiling, laughing, and having a wonderful time. I still have the thank-you notes they wrote me when they graduated from the class. Both promised to continue to be nice and to work hard. Yet they came to our school one afternoon armed with smoke bombs. They ran through the halls and threw the smoke bombs into classrooms, destroying property. They also detonated them on teachers' cars. Mine was the first one they chose. For weeks I didn't sleep well, trying to understand how they had become so lost in such a short time.

But that's what I do. It's what all good teachers and parents do. We ask a lot of our kids and do the best we can. We need to raise the bar for children precisely because so many kids are behaving so badly. We cannot allow incorrigible behavior to make us lower our standards. I refuse to go back to telling a child to do something because I said so. I will not trick myself into believing that if a student looks up to me I've accomplished something. I can't do that.

A few years ago, I missed a day of school in order to speak to a group of teachers in another state. As is my custom, I told my class in advance and did not discuss consequences if they behaved poorly for the substitute. I did not promise any rewards if they behaved well. I told them I'd miss them and would see them the day after my talk.

When I returned, I found a note from the substitute to the effect that my students were wonderful. I gave it a quick glance and began setting up for our day. About an hour later, during math, the kids were working quietly on some word problems involving fractions. There was a knock at the door of my classroom, and a short woman came in, holding hands with her six-year-old son. She spoke Spanish and asked if she could talk to me. Something had happened to her little boy, a first-grader, the day before. Walking home from school, he had been beaten up and robbed of his backpack. While this was happening, other students, as is so often the case, only watched or continued on their way home. But a little girl who was walking by had picked him off the sidewalk, taken him to a fountain, cleaned him up, and walked him home to make sure he arrived safely. The boy's mother was going around that morning trying to find the girl who had helped her son. She wanted to thank her.

I asked my class if anyone knew about this. Nobody knew anything. Having been absent the day before, I was clueless. I told the mom about some other classes to check and tried to comfort her little boy by telling him to remember that while there were mean kids in the world there was also a nice one who had helped him. They left and continued their search.

As I shut the door I noticed that most of the kids were talking to one another, speculating on which school bully had perpetrated the crime—some bullies seemed more likely than others. Out of the thirty-two kids in my class, thirty-one were involved in the discussion. Brenda kept working on her math, head bent closely over her paper. I noticed this because Brenda hated math. (She was a marvelous reader, and she used to joke with me that try as I might, I would never convince her of the beauty of arithmetic.)

I stared at her as she hunched over her math problems in the back corner of the room. And for one oh-so-brief moment she looked up, unaware that I was watching her. She looked up because she had a secret and wanted to know if anyone knew it. I didn't until our eyes met for a split second. Her eyes narrowed and she gave me a serious shake of her head that told me to mind my own business. "Don't ask me anything and don't give voice to your thoughts," her face told me before she put her head down and went back to work.

It was Brenda. She had helped the little boy, but her plan for anonymity had been foiled by the mother and my brief glance. I asked the other kids to get back to work and resumed my business. The rest of the day was a blur. Brenda had reached Level VI and no one would ever know. She and I have remained very close over the years, but we have never discussed that day.

I don't think we can do better than this.

PART TWO

THE METHOD

A Few Simple Ideas to Enhance

a Child's Development

THREE

Reading for Life

I t is 2:00 P.M. on a Tuesday, which means I am about to endure from one to two hours of torture. No, not thumbscrews and the rack—worse. It is time for the weekly staff meeting. I have struggled for years to convey to outsiders just how horrible these sessions are. Recently, a fellow teacher and friend helped me make the nature of our meetings understandable to others. He is battling cancer, and his chemotherapy treatments take place each Tuesday after the meeting. He told me he looks forward to chemotherapy because, he says, after the meeting, "the worst is over!"

I have suffered through staff meetings for years now, and, like many other teachers, I have adopted various measures to ease the pain. My fellow teachers and I have mastered the art of seeming to pay attention while some administrator out of Orwell's Ministry of Truth announces the current misinformation. One day, I almost broke down and had a seizure. I am not ashamed to admit this. Senator John McCain, who survived imprisonment and torture during the Vietnam War, could not endure the torture we withstand in these meetings.

You see, the children at our school do not read well. They do not like to read. As of this writing, 78 percent of the Latino children on our campus are not proficient in reading, according to our state's standardized tests. This means one of two things: Either we have the stupidest kids on the planet, or we are failing these children. Please believe me when I tell you that the vast majority of our students are perfectly capable of learning to read. No one wants to admit it, but a systemic conspiracy of mediocrity keeps these children on the treadmill of illiteracy.

To fight the problem, we now have "literacy coaches" at school. Most of these "experts" are former classroom teachers who never accomplished much with their own students. At one staff development meeting, a supervisor of these literacy coaches came in to inspire us to help Johnny read. She began her talk sagely by holding up a rather large book between her thumb and forefinger, as if it was a turd. She laughed a knowing laugh and told us, "We all know our students would never want to read a big, fat book." The volume she held up with disdain was John Steinbeck's *The Grapes of Wrath,* a book that won the Pulitzer Prize by an author who won a Nobel Prize.

Teaching our children to read well and helping them develop a love of reading should be our top priorities. People seem to under-

stand this. Millions are spent on books and other reading material, celebrities make public service announcements, and thousands of hours are spent training teachers. The spin doctors at various publishing companies tell us that our students are doing better, but honest people know this is simply not the case. Concerned teachers have learned not to bother raising their voices, because powerful textbook companies have carefully prepared answers to anyone who points out that the emperor has no clothes. Young teachers are afraid of being crushed by bureaucrats whose only real mission is to keep selling their product. As testing services compete to rake in millions of dollars, nervous school districts anxiously await the latest test results. And year after year, most children do not become passionate lifelong readers.

It's complicated. There is a lot of finger-pointing. But to borrow a phrase from another big, fat book that won a Pulitzer Prize, our children are victims of a sort of "confederacy of dunces." Powerful forces of mediocrity have combined to prevent perfectly competent children from learning to love reading. These forces include television, video games, poor teaching, poverty, the breakup of the family, and a general lack of adult guidance.

I am not oblivious to the challenges that many good and caring administrators face. The teachers they supervise are often apathetic or incompetent or both. As a result, districts have turned to monotonous shared reading texts and have ordered all teachers to teach the same material at the same pace to all students. We're supposed to follow the script. Such directives come with robotic automatons whose purpose is to make sure teachers are following the program. Of course many bad teachers benefit from such regimentation. But good teachers do not. We are no longer supposed to introduce our students to powerful, challenging works of literature. We are punished for the incompetence of some teachers. The real losers, however, are the kids.

No one has all the answers. Not all of my students develop a love of reading. But all of them improve and most of them have an exciting year reading with me. Some succumb to the aforementioned forces when they leave my class, but many become hooked for life. Here are some strategies that I use in Room 56. I hope you'll find an idea or two that might be useful in raising your child or running your classroom.

A Different Focus

Schools have lost sight of why we read. Like many school communities, the Los Angeles Unified School District uses scripted basal readers to teach children to read. A glance at the district's list of reading objectives explains why students do not find this reading material exciting. The objectives always focus on fluency, comprehension, and other necessary but deadly dull goals. I have never seen district reading objectives in which the words *joy, passion,* or *excitement* top the list. I think they should.

These are the reasons why readers read, and we've lost sight of this fact. I read every day, and it is not because of a test coming up or because I want my achievement scores printed in the paper to demonstrate that my school is improving. I read because I like to read. Friends share their favorite new books with me and can't wait to hear my reaction. I read about good books in the newspaper, hear about good books on the radio, or overhear strangers discussing their new favorites in a public place. I was the same way as a child. I'm no genius, but I'm a reasonably good reader, and never as a child was I put through thousands of hours of reading testing to assess my progress. I spent those hours reading great books. Those books made me hungry for more books. My appetite for literature and trips to the library were a better assessment of my progress than any standardized test.

My fifth-graders laugh because they made up their own reading test consisting of only three questions. According to them, it is a far more accurate test of reading proficiency than anything designed by some testing service.

1. Have you ever secretly read under your desk in school because the teacher was boring and you were dying to finish the book you were reading?
2. Have you ever been scolded for reading at the dinner table?
3. Have you ever read secretly under the covers after being told to go to bed?

My students and I agree that if a child answers yes to all three questions, he or she is destined to become a reader for life.

I want my students to love to read. Reading is not a subject. Reading is a foundation of life, an activity that people who are engaged with the world do all the time. It is often exceedingly difficult to convince young people of this fact, given the world in which they are growing up. But it is possible, and when you consider what is at stake, the effort is worth it. If a child is going to grow into a truly special adult—someone who thinks, considers other points of view, has an open mind, and possesses the ability to discuss great ideas with other people—a love of reading is an essential foundation.

The Adult as Guide

During a recent trip to Washington, D.C., my class and I ate lunch at the Smithsonian Museum of American History. The museum's food court has a broad variety of selections. It's a good place for the kids to eat a healthful meal and refresh themselves before spending more time in the museum.

A terrific boy named Timmy had not been feeling well. The evening before he had been up all night with vomiting and diarrhea. In the morning he had felt strong enough to go to the museum, and indeed he seemed to be recovering. As we walked into the food court for lunch, I pulled him aside.

Rafe: *How ya feeling, buddy?*

Timmy: *A little weak, but I'm okay, Rafe.*

Rafe: *That's great. I think you know you need to be careful about what you eat.*

Timmy: *What do you think?*

Rafe: *Well, no sodas today, Timmy. Let's stick to bland stuff like soups, veggies, and bread until you're feeling a hundred percent, okay?*

Timmy: *Okay!*

I watched my students get their trays and begin choosing their meals. Some were getting chicken, some pizza, and still others were choosing salads. I had to laugh: Timmy had skipped all the entrée lines and was placing a huge brownie on his tray next to the two chocolate chip cookies he had already selected. I intercepted him at the beverage cooler, where he was reaching for a chocolate milk. Now, Timmy is a wonderfully bright kid and I love having him in class. But he's ten years old. He needs to be guided. I took the junk food off his hands and helped him make some wiser selections. He soon felt better and went on to have a good day.

Children—even very bright ones—need guidance. Whether they are selecting food or literature, kids need our leadership to help them find the right path.

I am not smarter than my students. But I know more than they do because I am older than they are. I know about fabulous books that they might not yet have come across. It is my job as their mentor to put these books in their hands. Because the kids trust me, they are more likely to try a book I suggest. If one of my students is a *Harry Potter* fan, it's easy to introduce him to other wonderful fantasy books. The joy of hearing one of the children laugh out loud while reading *The Phantom Tollbooth* or ask if she can borrow the next installment of *The Chronicles of Narnia* remains a thrill for me. I get chills watching their minds try to comprehend the layers upon layers of *Alice in Wonderland*. Sharing the joy of great literature can be a cornerstone of a relationship between an adult and a child. It is through literature that young people first begin to look at the world differently, to open their minds to new ideas, to journey down an avenue of excellence. To complete the metaphor: Reading nothing but basal readers often leads to a dead end.

Occasionally, I use books on CD. I've noticed that the kids find two recordings particularly engaging: *The Autobiography of Malcolm X* (read by actor Joe Morton) and *Anne Frank: The Diary of a Young Girl* (read by Winona Ryder). Each of these classic memoirs is told in the first person, and hearing a professional voice tell the story helps to hook the kids. With certain books, this approach is more effective than having students trade off reading sections.

There is a danger here, however. I have seen teachers play a book on CD and take a break. This is tantamount to using a television as a babysitter. It takes a master teacher to use an audio book effectively. A good teacher always stops the CD at intervals, either to make sure the kids understand a point or to lead a discussion on a crucial issue. This is especially important when listening to difficult material. It takes practice, though; stopping the flow too often can kill the students' concentration and enjoyment. I always have in mind places to stop the CD, and I monitor my students meticulously to make sure they understand what they're hearing.

At the Library

Parents need to take their kids to the library. For many families this has become a vanishing activity. With the rise of home shopping on the Internet, more and more kids order books online. It's wonderful that children are ordering books, but it is not as meaningful as going to the library. We are trying to establish a set of values in our children; it helps when they are surrounded by others who share a fervor for reading. At the library, children can browse and make discoveries that wouldn't be possible online; at the same time they can interact with readers of all ages instead of just opening a package that shows up in their mailbox. These days, children who read are often mocked by ignorant peers. But when a kid who makes a weekly trip to the library is told, "Nobody reads anymore," he knows it's not true. He can think to himself, *Maybe no one* you *know reads, pal, but I know you are mistaken.* The best way to combat the indifference that surrounds our children is to take them to places where intelligence, enthusiasm, and a joy for reading are standard operating procedure. The library is the best place to begin.

But our job is not done once we walk in the library door. Adults must serve as guides. One day, my students and I were in our school library when a group of about twenty fifth-graders rumbled noisily into the room. I looked up and noticed they were unsupervised.

The group spent about thirty minutes in the library. Some went online and looked at Web sites that had nothing to do with reading. Some sat and talked with friends. Others looked for books with no supervision or guidance. Like so many tragic moments, this was a scene of missed opportunity. Here were students losing out on a chance to find books that might help them discover the joy of reading. Instead, most returned to class with books they had already read or no book at all. Their teacher was still on the phone when they returned. The schedule in their room noted that the children had gone to the library.

Choosing Literature

There are many ways to find terrific books for children. Of course the simplest way is to share books you love and continue to enjoy. But if you are looking for a place to start, type "Newbery Award" into Google and peruse the list of terrific novels that have won the award over the years. I have yet to find an elementary school child who has not discovered the joy of reading when presented with such classics as *Bridge to Terabithia*, *The Westing Game*, or *Number the Stars*.

A list of Caldecott Award winners is a good place to begin when searching for books for very young readers. Librarians also have all sorts of lists from which both parents and teachers can begin their quest to find books that will be remembered forever.

You may be an elementary-school teacher whose district guidelines force you to use some terrible basal reading series and discourage reading great literature in its entirety. Many reading companies falsely claim it is not necessary to read entire books because there are samples of fine prose in the chapters that fill up their texts. They do not want classroom teachers reading literature with their students because doing so might mean that schools would stop ordering the countless addenda and "new, improved" versions of their run-of-the-mill selections.

The argument that placing portions of literature within basal readers is good enough for our children is laughable. Just last year I witnessed what can result from this strategy. Our school uses a school text whose selections include a fragment of *Anne Frank: The Diary of a Young Girl.* A young teacher at the school attempted to do the right thing. Knowing that *Anne Frank* was an important work, he obtained a class set of books and told his students to read the book during their winter vacation and to be prepared for a test when they returned. The result was a disaster. The students were too young to understand anything in the book. They were given no background on World War II and couldn't even find the Netherlands on a map. Seemingly incomprehensible abbreviations and words like *BBC* and *menstruation* turned off even this teacher's most diligent students. When they later came to my class, they moaned when I told them *Anne Frank* was on our reading list.

This is the worst example of what can happen when basal readers, good intentions, and poor guidance are combined: The kids not only hadn't appreciated this historic chronicle, but had developed an intense hatred of it! Fortunately, with patience I was able to undo the damage and show the students why Anne's story will live forever. But wouldn't it have been better if these children had been guided through this important work in a meaningful way in the first place?

I would not advise young teachers to fight the powers that be. The only result of your reasonable push for literature will be to have more administrators and coaches in your room interfering with your worthy efforts to get kids to read. Rather than waste energy on a fight that cannot be won, play the game and follow the school plan. But all is not lost. The challenge is to find other times in the day to read fantastic books. Start a book club during your lunch hour or after school. Of course this is difficult and time-consuming, and it is absurd that a good young teacher should need to work extra hours and battle bureaucrats to allow her students to read great literature. But when one considers the stakes, no price is too high.

Students Who Cannot Read

Many teachers would love to read literature with their students but have some students who struggle with challenging works. Fearing the idea of leaving a child behind, teachers often use less demanding material to help such students feel they are succeeding. The result is that capable and exceptional students are bored out of their minds waiting for others to catch up.

I use a two-pronged strategy here. First, by constantly explaining material, I am able to keep struggling students up to speed. I prepare in advance particularly simple passages for students who are beginning readers. I create their success before the lesson even begins. They gain confidence on a daily basis because they read in front of their peers, are never laughed at when they struggle, and find themselves improving faster than they ever had in the past. When I assign written work, I am there to help such students answer questions and improve their writing skills.

The second part of my reading strategy is to have individual kids read books associated with their particular reading levels. Each month they write reports on these books. This activity will be covered in greater detail in chapter 4.

By guiding the students and helping them overcome their insecurities, I help even my lowest-achieving students gain confidence. They are being challenged in an environment that combines a push for excellence with a nurturing, positive mentor. Last year all of my students who came to me with a rating of "far below basic" passed their basic reading proficiency tests at the end of the year.

Middle and High School Teachers

One of the misconceptions young people have today is that reading is something we study only during English class. This notion is absurd and must be countered. I've found that one of the best ways to do this is for all teachers to start book clubs. Where is it written that math or science teachers should not be reading role models for their students?

I've seen any number of marvelous science, history, and physical education teachers run book clubs. They select a good book and give all the kids in their various classes the option of reading it. Most of these clubs have scheduled meetings, often during the lunch hour or after school. After completing a chapter, the group meets to discuss it. The students participate voluntarily, so the teacher is working with enthusiastic young people. The kids get to meet like-minded peers from other classes whom they might not have gotten to know otherwise. Friendships are formed. The teacher bonds with young scholars in a different environment, which strengthens the teacher-student relationship in the classroom. It is a superb way for all involved to spend a couple of hours a week. Everyone wins. It's reading for all the right reasons.

Parents can do the same thing at home. Some have a family reading hour, while others ask everyone to read, say, chapter 2 of *Great Expectations* by dinner on Thursday. Our children need to have adults constantly reading and discussing books with them. We need to be the people we want our children to become.

Assessment

Most parents and teachers agree that when a skill is being taught, there needs to be an assessment to see if proficiency has been achieved. Discussion is never enough. How can we check for understanding when our children are reading good literature?

Both parents and teachers can go to a Web site called www. learninglinks.com. This company offers a series of study guides called Novel-ties, which I find to be excellent supplements to reading. I should note that other companies offer similar guides. The Novel-ties guides cover hundreds of books by a variety of authors, from Beverly Cleary to Mark Twain. Each study guide features chapter-by-chapter vocabulary lessons to teach new words and help students better understand the material they are reading. Students are asked to use the new words in analogies and other word games to take ownership of their new knowledge. Students also write essays and answer comprehension questions that relate to the novel.

As a parent and teacher, my time is incredibly limited. Given my schedule, I cannot possibly prepare dozens of comprehension questions for each chapter I read with students. Novel-ties solve the problem. They are well organized and, most important of all, reach for the highest levels of understanding. They never "dumb down" the material. By using the workbooks, my students become better readers, writers, and thinkers.

Making Things Relevant

I am constantly astonished to hear the range of reasons why students are reading what they're reading: "My teacher assigned it because it's on the list." "There are questions on the test that refer to this book." "I need to read this to pass the course." All of these far-too-frequent answers fall wide of the mark in terms of why we want our children to be readers.

Young people who read for pleasure are able to make connections with the world around them and eventually grow to understand themselves on levels they never thought possible. They make associations between characters and situations that can shape their own decisions. When my ten-year-old students performed both parts of *Henry IV* in one night, many cynics questioned their ability to find meaning in the antics of Prince Hal and Falstaff. The children knew better. In scrutinizing Prince Hal's struggle to find honor in a dishonorable world, they learned something about how to approach their own struggles in the cafeteria and on the playground.

Not a year goes by that a great piece of literature is not filmed or performed on a local stage. Parents and teachers need to be on the lookout for such adaptations, which are best enjoyed after a reading of the work being adapted. If we can guide students to a film or a performance of a work they have read, it can lead to a discussion about how close the production came to their own experience of the work. In recent years, films have been made of *The Lord of the Rings*, *The Chronicles of Narnia*, *Of Mice and Men*, and many other great works of literature. Local theaters produce plays by writers from Oscar Wilde to William Inge to August Wilson. When children read books knowing they will also watch an adaptation on the screen or stage and be asked to compare the two experiences, they pursue their reading with far more passion and vigor than if their only purpose is to pass a test. This should be the goal for our children.

Laughter and Tears

We parents and teachers must remember that despite the state of our culture, it is still possible to develop lifelong readers. Many of my students are living proof. But in the age of cable television, DVDs, video games, and the Internet, it has never been more difficult. This fact must not discourage us. As Shakespeare wrote in *Measure for Measure*:

> Our doubts are traitors,
> And make us lose the good we oft might win
> By fearing to attempt.

If we do make the attempt, we may have a student like Luis. Like many of my students, Luis volunteered to participate in a Saturday class I teach for former students who miss Room 56 and want to keep this haven as a part of their lives. These middle and high school kids practice for the SAT, read literature, and prepare for college.

One Saturday we were reading Lorraine Hansberry's classic play *A Raisin in the Sun*. In a few weeks we would take a field trip to the Shakespeare festival in Ashland, Oregon, where we would see Hansberry's play and many others, and I wanted the kids to be prepared. I took the time to find copies of the play and guide the students through it while providing context on how it changed the face of American theater. As we read the final lines of the play, many students sighed with the joy and contentment that comes with finishing a masterpiece. But Luis sat there with tears rolling down his cheeks. No one laughed at this fourteen-year-old student as he choked back the sobs. When he had regained his composure, I asked him what moved him so deeply about the play. His answer was simple. "I am crying," he said, "because this is *my* family."

He is a reader. He makes connections. He understands. He is able to investigate great ideas and see their relevance to his own experience. It may very well be that years from now a young student will be reading something Luis has written.

This I believe: If young people develop a love of reading, they will have better lives. That objective is not listed in our state curriculum standards. Our assessment of reading may begin with standardized test scores, but in the end we must measure a child's reading ability by the amount of laughter exhaled and tears shed as the written word is devoured. Laughter and tears may not be listed in the state curriculum of reading objectives, but they are the standard in Room 56. These kids read for life.

FOUR

Writing

I n general, students today are very poor writers, and it's no wonder. Given the cumulative effect of lack of practice, poor teaching, text messaging, e-mail jargon, and a culture that practically celebrates illiteracy, it should come as no surprise that the majority of students cannot write even a cohesive paragraph, let alone an essay or report. Consider the following:

1982   In my first year of teaching, the school provides my class with beautiful new grammar books. They are well organized and quite thorough. The explanations and examples are clear. By the end of the year, the children will have a solid understanding of parts of speech, sentence structure, and good writing. In addition, several outstanding teachers introduce me to a project called Young Authors, which gives every child in the Los Angeles Unified School District the opportunity to write his or her own book. The students spend the year writing, illustrating, and binding spectacular stories. These books are then presented at a conference at a local college, where thousands and thousands of students come on a Saturday to enjoy the books. Prizes are awarded to the best.

1990   The school is ordering books on various subjects. At a meeting, many good teachers point out that our grammar books are getting a little worn after eight years of use. Perhaps we need to order new ones, as we do with math and science. None are ordered. By this time the Young Authors program has been canceled. It is too time-consuming for the organizers. Schools are encouraged to have their own Young Authors Days.

1994   My school's leaders are not happy with our own Young Authors Day. Some teachers are not having their class write books. Other teachers are submitting books from previous years. We attend a staff development meeting at which veteran teachers show the newer ones how to create exciting Young Authors books.

1997   The district becomes even more obsessed than usual with administering standardized tests. Teachers are overloaded with testing days. Educators will spend approximately 30 out of 163 days giving district and state tests. Instructors understandably moan, "How can I teach anything when I am given no time to teach?"

1998   At a staff meeting, the teachers vote to cancel our Young Authors Day. Instead, each child will write a Young Author book and show it to his or her parents on Back-to-School Night. During this meeting, other school activities are thrown out as well: science fair, spelling bee, geography bee, and Dr. King Day celebrations. At least teachers still have the terrific grammar books, old and tattered as they have become.

2000   Our school adopts a new basal reading series. We are as-
        signed two literacy coaches to help the teachers. One of the
        many jobs of the literacy coaches is to remove the grammar
        books from classrooms. Teachers are told they may teach
        grammar only from the new materials. Instructors complain
        that while the new series does indeed address parts of speech
        and sentence structure, the older grammar books do a far
        better job. Teachers are told they must surrender the gram-
        mar books anyway. We ask if we can compromise and use
        the grammar books as a supplement to the official school
        texts. This is not allowed. Frightened younger teachers turn
        in their books. Some clever older instructors hide the books
        or share one series among themselves and teach their stu-
        dents good grammar secretly.

2001   At a staff development meeting, we learn something new
        about teaching reading and writing: When we grade the
        district-mandated writing assignments, we are no longer to
        count misspelled words as wrong. This way, we can sup-
        posedly get a more "accurate" assessment of our students'
        progress.

2003   As part of the basal reading and language series, students
        are now required to take a test every six weeks in which
        they stand next to their teacher and read two selections
        out loud as quickly as they possibly can. Many teachers ques-
        tion the reasoning behind this, and point out that in our
        own lives we never read out loud for speed. Still, charts
        are posted in the school hallways to record the competition
        among different grades and tracks to see who reads the
        fastest.

2004	After three years of using the new basal reading series, our school's reading scores are not improving. In fact, in many areas they are down. Our third-grade reading scores are dismal.

For three years we have been told on a weekly basis that the key to reading is fluency. We are now informed by the "Ministry of Truth," a.k.a. the literacy coaches, that we were wrong to place so much importance on the fluency test. It has always been the *comprehension test* that matters. We are told not to worry about our mistaken perception of past meetings. The fluency charts are taken down in the school hallway. Hmmm . . . *Yes, comrades, we have never been at war with Oceania.*

Later in the year, students are asked to take another district writing test. They will write about a topic that bores them silly. It will take two days to complete. The teacher in charge of distributing the tests has my exams delivered to our classroom. They come with the following note from the teacher: "Hear our you're exams, Rafe. Their due Friday."

We teachers and parents have our work cut out for us. Despite these hurdles and roadblocks, we need to find strategies and activities that help children become better writers. Francis Bacon wrote, "Reading maketh a full man, Conference a ready man, and Writing an exact man." I want my students to be able to express themselves with precision. I want them to write well not because of the test coming up, but because writing well will help them for the rest of their lives, whether they are applying for college or a job. Here now are four things I do with my students to improve their writing:

Step I. Start Me Up: Grammar

Our school day officially begins at 8:00 A.M. Although the majority of my class voluntarily begins school earlier than this, all of my students are in their seats by then. A grammar assignment is already on the board and worksheets are on their desks (the books have been confiscated, but it is easy to find workbooks of grammar exercises at any teacher supply store).

Each morning begins with a grammar exercise. Perhaps the students are asked to identify proper nouns or to choose the correct verb tense for a sentence. Before attendance is taken, before homework is collected, before the kids have a chance to even consider being distracted, they are working on grammar. I do take a moment to wish them good morning and tell them we have an exciting day planned, but by 8:01 we are hard at work while other students saunter by our door. We do not waste time in Room 56. Even a few squandered minutes at the start of the day can add up to twenty or thirty hours over the course of a year. Our children cannot afford such waste.

They work hard for three reasons. First, many of the students come to enjoy grammar. All of my students speak English as a second language, and they appreciate learning to write their new language correctly. They see themselves improve and, because they feel comfortable in Room 56, they do not worry about making mistakes. They know no one will laugh at them or scold them.

The second reason is to avoid having to take work home. In class, the kids are given thirty minutes to answer twenty questions. After I teach the skill for five or so minutes, and check to make sure the kids understand it, they have perhaps twenty-three minutes to finish. Whatever questions are left will be assigned as homework, so they have learned that it is always better to finish work in class. Here they have peers and their teacher to consult when questions arise, and the classroom is almost always more conducive to quality work than home, with siblings screaming and television sets blasting.

Most important of all, the kids want to do this work because of what we call the "Dreaded Rewrite." This idea arose from hearing former students complain that in most classes, when they turned in an assignment of any kind, one of three things happened: It was either returned with a good grade or a poor grade or, most often, not returned at all. In Room 56, rather than receive poor grades, my students are told they must get at least 90 percent or better on grammar assignments or do them again. They are not punished, disgraced, or any such thing. They simply have to do the assignment over and over until they have mastered the skill. At the beginning of the year, practically every child in the class rewrites his or her grammar on a daily basis. By the second week, only two or three students need to redo work each day. The Dreaded Rewrite makes kids understand that Room 56 is a serious place and they might as well listen, try hard, ask questions, and get things right the first time.

The next morning, as the students work on their new grammar assignments, my graders come around and pick up the previous day's work. At recess, the graders quickly and accurately correct the papers and prepare a list of Dreaded Rewrites. The list is posted at the front of the room and is greeted with delirious sighs and cries of exultation by the many students who have done their work correctly. My favorite part of all this comes a few minutes later, after the exhilaration or despair is over, when the students who mastered the skills are sitting right alongside those who did not, helping the less fortunate with the problems they missed and encouraging them to succeed that night and the next day.

Steps II and III. Essay of the Week
and Monthly Book Report

The next two writing exercises arose from mistakes I made in my younger days. As an elementary-school teacher, I had frequent conversations with former pupils now attending middle or high school. They missed Room 56 and would tell me what I was doing well and, more important, what I could do to improve. One of my many mistakes was not helping the children understand the importance of time management. All of the homework assignments in my class were given one day and due the next. My recent graduates thought it would be helpful for some assignments to be due at the end of the week or even the month. In this way, students could learn to begin work on such projects before they piled up.

Enter the Essay of the Week and the Monthly Book Report. These two projects are harder to assign, grade, and teach than the grammar exercises, but they teach the value of time management while simultaneously improving the students' writing.

Essay of the Week

Each Friday, I assign the Essay of the Week. These short essays, usually about a page long, run the gamut from serious to silly. One week the children may be asked to weigh in on George's decision to kill Lennie in *Of Mice and Men*. The following week the students may write a page on how they would spend twenty-four hours if they swallowed a potion that made them invisible. In all cases, the students are asked to write with proper grammar, spelling, sentence structure, and organization. I want their writing to be—as Francis Bacon says—*precise.*

These essays are assigned on Friday and collected a week later for two specific reasons. First, it gives the kids the opportunity to write on the weekend. They don't have to do this, of course. I encourage them to spend lots of time with family and friends, playing ball, relaxing, and having the silliest kinds of fun. But even if they spend only an hour or two writing on the weekend, they still have dozens of hours for play. The Essay of the Week gives students the opportunity to practice balancing work with play.

Second, it gives me the weekend to give student work the time it deserves. There is no way for me to adequately correct essays on a school night. With so many lessons to prepare for the next day, and my family to care for, I am too tired and busy to do the essays justice. By Monday morning, my students have their work back with helpful comments. I must show them I care about their writing if I expect them to care as well.

Over the weekend I do something else I've found to be extremely effective. I choose a few of their essays and type them up exactly as I received them, mistakes and all. On Monday morning, instead of a grammar assignment of the day, the students read two or three essays from the previous week. The names are removed from the papers to avoid embarrassment.

Within weeks the kids grow enormously as writers. By looking at a range of student essays, they start to see why some are better than others. By the end of the year, my fifth-graders rarely make mistakes in spelling, grammar, or structure, and they even master many finer points of writing, such as avoiding dangling modifiers. I have done nothing to make them smarter—I'm not a good enough teacher to do that. But by constantly writing and evaluating one another's work, the kids become better writers, and they have a good time getting there.

As a class, we never miss an opportunity to evaluate writing. In fact, during the writing of this book a colleague of mine was furious with me. She thought I had let her down by not helping one of her students with a problem. One morning the phone rang in my room and she screamed at me before hanging up. At lunch, I found a note in my box. Well, let's be precise—it was more a hate letter than a note, and it informed me that, among other things, I blow and suck.

I could have written back, but I had a better use for the note. I made copies for the kids and had them evaluate the writing. They gave it high marks for passion but thought it needed work on tone. I declined their idea of making some notes and returning it to the teacher.

The Monthly Book Report

Like the Essay of the Week, monthly book reports are an effective way to help students learn time management while simultaneously improving their writing skills. Of course, no single "book report model" will work for all classrooms and students. This is what Room 56 does each month. It works well for us, and a variation could work well for you.

For the book reports, I have the children read easy books; the titles we read in class are too difficult for many of them to handle individually. I provide a set of Newbery award winners and other simple but first-rate novels, and each student chooses a new book at the beginning of the month. A kid who struggles with reading might pick a very easy book by Beverly Cleary. All of the novels on this list have one thing in common: They are marvelous books that are beloved by children because they are so much fun to read. Whether a student is reading *The Phantom Tollbooth, Beezus and Ramona,* or *Mr. Popper's Penguins,* every child is reading a wonderful book at all times.

Our monthly book reports are divided into short sections, each of which is devoted to a different element of the novel: the protagonist, antagonist, conflict, setting, plot, climax, denouement, and theme. To help the kids understand these difficult concepts, I show them *The Wizard of Oz* (which the majority of my students have never heard of!).

I use *Oz* because the story is so clear it allows the kids to quickly understand the concepts. Dorothy is the protagonist and the Wicked Witch the antagonist. The conflict is person versus person (as opposed to person vs. nature, himself, or society). The setting is a Kansas farm and the Land of Oz. The climax is the moment when the Wicked Witch gets hit by water ("I'm melting!"). The denouement comes when Dorothy and her friends resolve their situations: the Scarecrow gets his brains, the Tin Man his heart, the Cowardly Lion his courage, and Dorothy returns home. Of course the theme is easy enough for the children to identify, because Dorothy repeats it so many times: "There's no place like home."

Next, the class reads its first book of the year together—usually Ellen Raskin's *The Westing Game*. It's a terrifically funny children's murder mystery, and my class gets a big kick out of it. Then I hand out a "book report" of the novel. This lets the kids see exactly what I expect of them when they write their first report on the book they have chosen for the month.

Of course, the kids will make all sorts of mistakes on their first book reports. Even with an example to follow, they make numerous errors in spelling, grammar, tense, and sentence structure. They also make analytical errors. They often identify the wrong character as the protagonist (e.g., Lennie instead of George in *Of Mice and Men*) or tell the entire story rather than summarizing the plot. But that's okay. It's only the first time they've tried it. I take at least a week to go over these book reports. In the meantime, the kids begin working on their next report. By the time they get their first papers back and see what they could have done better, they are able to use my comments to improve their second papers. After a year of this, my students generally turn in excellent papers and have read ten or twelve good books in the process.

Still another advantage of monthly book reports is that they eliminate the comment "I'm done," often uttered by a lone student during a history or math assignment:

Rafe: *Really, John? Have you finished your book, and are you ready to hand in your monthly book report?*

John: (Sheepishly) *Uh, no. Guess I better get to work on that.*

Monthly book reports are not easy for teachers or parents. It can be a challenge to select books that children find captivating, and it takes time to grade the reports and provide helpful feedback. But your kids will grow as readers, writers, and critical thinkers when this happens. It's hard work but it's worth it.

Here is a book report that was written by one of my fifth-graders:

THE ADVENTURES OF TOM SAWYER

by Mark Twain

Protagonist

Tom Sawyer is the protagonist of the novel. He is about 12 years old and lives in the small town of St. Petersburg, Missouri. He wants to be an outlaw and likes to play hooky from school and church. He drives his Aunt Polly crazy, and hates his half brother Sid.

Antagonist

Injun Joe is the antagonist of this story. Joe is a half breed Indian and a robber and murderer. He kills Dr. Robinson and in addition plans a brutal attack on a wealthy widow. He is greedy and bitter because of his treatment by the townspeople.

Conflict

This is a person vs. person conflict. Tom wants to get the $12,000 Joe has stolen, and Joe wants to kill the Widow Douglas and then get away. Both characters cannot get what they want, so there is a conflict.

Setting

The story takes place in a small town in Missouri during the 1830's. The setting is very important to the story because the town represents the place where Mark Twain grew up. Many of the characters are based on people he actually knew. The language, superstitions, and culture of the village are all important in this story.

Plot

Tom Sawyer is a mischievous and hilarious boy growing up in the 1830's by the Mississippi River. He is constantly in trouble with his Aunt Polly, who loves him and suffers trying to raise him. Tom is a very clever boy. He tricks his friends into whitewashing the fence, and wins a Bible in church by cheating his friends out of their prize tickets.

Tom is not a good student, and often plays hooky. He likes girls, and leaves Amy Lawrence for Becky Thatcher. His best friends are Joe Harper and Huck Finn. Huck is the son of the town drunk and disliked by all the adults. The kids respect him because he is the only free boy in town.

Tom, Joe, and Huck plan many adventures. One time they run away from home and camp on Jackson Island. The town believes the boys are dead, and are in for an amazing surprise when the boys return and show up at their own funeral.

One night, the boys go to a graveyard with a dead cat to try to cure warts. They accidentally witness Injun Joe killing Doc Robinson. Muff Potter, a kindly drunk, gets blamed for the murder. At the trial, Tom testifies and Potter is saved. However, Joe escapes and Tom spends sleepless nights worrying Joe will come to kill him.

One day Huck and Tom look for buried treasure. They stumble upon a "haunted" house, and discover Joe and his partner hiding their stolen money. There is over $12,000 in coins. The boys plan to follow the thieves and steal the money for themselves.

Becky Thatcher plans a picnic. One of the activities is for the children to explore a cave. After the picnic ends, the children go home, not knowing that Tom and Becky have been left behind and are lost in the cave. Their lives are in danger. Tom also discovers Joe hiding in the cave.

Tom eventually escapes. The town has bolted the cave shut, not knowing that in doing so they are killing Injun Joe. Tom and Huck become heroes, and with Joe's treasure are now rich and famous.

Climax
The climax of the book is when Injun Joe dies. Tom says after the trial he will never sleep well until he sees Joe dead.

He gets his wish when the people reenter the cave and find Joe's body. Tom will never be bothered again by this man.

Denouement
At the end of the story, Tom tells the town that he and Huck are rich. The boys shock the people by bringing in a wagon with $12,000. Huck will live with the Widow Douglas, and Tom will be a town hero.

Theme
Mark Twain writes himself that the theme is for adults to remember what it was to be a child. The book makes fun of how silly children can be, and reminds us of the fun they can have before having to enter "civilization."

This is not a perfect report, yet it is an excellent start for a fifth-grade child who speaks English as a second language. There are countless ways for kids to write about books, but my students have found this form to be thorough, challenging, and effective.

Step IV. Paperback Writer: The Young Authors Project

Young Authors projects are not for the faint of heart. They are hard to pull off, take massive amounts of time and patience, and can be exhausting. But I will let you in on a little secret: I have students from twenty years ago who completed hundreds of assignments for me, and the only things they have kept after all these years are their Young Authors books. They are important to the children.

The idea itself is not complicated. Basically, each student is given a year to write a book. There is more than one way to accomplish this, but I can share with you what has worked for Room 56. Here are a few dos and don'ts.

The students should write most of their books during class. This ensures the work is being done by the children and not by overanxious parents, siblings, or family friends. It also encourages the children to take their time. If they are asked to write their stories over a vacation period, they invariably rush to finish them the last night or two of the break. And from the teacher's perspective, it is impractical to be handed thirty or so stories, some of which might be twenty or thirty pages long, in one lump. You will *never* find the time to give the stories the attention they deserve.

I give my students thirty- to forty-five-minute chunks of time two or three afternoons a week in which to write their books. During each session I meet with five or six children. I ask each child to tell me what he is writing about. He shows me what he has written. This way, I can help him with grammar and spelling mistakes as the book is being written. It's the "ounce of prevention is worth a pound of cure" school of editing. I also talk with the writer about his characters. Too many kids write about what happened and forget that the best stories generally revolve around characters we care about. I make sure the forest is indeed a magical place but remind the kids to write about the characters who go into that forest.

From time to time I divide the class into small groups of three or four children who share their stories and edit one another's writing. This is good for all of us. The editors learn about writing by helping others get better. The writers get helpful advice. And I save time because many sloppy mistakes are cleaned up before the final stories are turned in.

Most teachers set some ground rules about the subject matter of these stories—lines that students are not allowed to cross. Some do not let their students write gory stories. Others make sure that no child ends his story with "and then they woke up and it was all a dream." The important thing is to be flexible and to use what you learn as you go forward.

During the editing process, you can encourage the kids to use figurative language. If a child writes that a character was scared, ask him, "How scared was he? Was he as afraid as a balloon near a porcupine?" Show the kids how much fun writing can be. It's a project, after all, not an assignment. It's different from test questions, Essays of the Week, or science experiments. Writing these books might be the only thing the children get to do with complete control—from the characters to the language to the plot twists. Remind the children that Shakespeare, Twain, Cervantes, and Steinbeck were once Young Authors, too. Your students could grow up to write the books that readers around the world will fall in love with.

Once the stories are completely written and edited, the kids type them into the computer, making sure they leave space throughout the text for illustrations. Drawings are done separately and pasted into the books. This way the children can attempt all sorts of drawings before settling on the perfect ones for the printed page. The kids come up with all kinds of creative pictures that pop up, unfold, or dazzle the reader.

When the books are ready to be bound, some teachers simply take them to Kinko's, which is fine, but I prefer to do the binding in class. The kids use heavy cardboard for the book covers and create bindings with Con-Tact paper, glue, and masking tape. It's always a lot of work, but I've found that the kids appreciate seeing the project through to the end.

At the end of the day, however—let's be realistic—writing may be the most difficult subject to teach. Given the enormous amount of time and energy it takes, combined with problems such as language barriers and absurd school policies, it is no wonder that so many good teachers have thrown in the towel and barely teach writing at all. I remember one December day when I was nodding off at my desk grading book reports. I opened a Christmas card from a student that said "Mery Kirstmas Raft." I guess my first five months with him hadn't made much of a difference.

But if you don't give up, writing might just be the key that unlocks a child's heart. We want to make connections with our children. Sometimes we build bridges playing catch, reading, or solving problems. Yet it is the power of the written word that might change a life. Children often write things they may feel too shy to express publicly. One girl I had wrote a story about her red ball. The ball had a happy face on it, and she and the ball played every day. One time her ball bounced over a fence and rolled down the street. The ball got covered in mud and now wore a sad face, as did the little girl in the story. The next day the girl's father drove down the street and saw the sad ball lying in the mud. In the author's words, "Her daddy saw it but was too lazy to pick it up."

Ouch! Here was a little girl who needed some love and attention, but I would have never known it without reading her story. She was a quiet and beautiful girl who was so painfully shy she was afraid to leave the classroom and play in the yard. It was her story that inspired me to be the man who would take the time to pick up the ball, clean it, and return it to her. We had a wonderful year together, and I gave her a red ball for graduation. We are still close twenty years later. She is a lawyer today, and her Young Author book about the red ball sits on her shelf with the law books in her office.

FIVE

Add It Up

The study of numbers is a polarizing subject. Kids (and adults) love it or hate it. Very few students shrug their shoulders with a neutral opinion when asked how they feel about math.

In urban elementary schools like the one where I teach, test scores follow a predictable pattern. Many students speak English as a second language and score poorly on reading tests but fare better in math. There's no mystery here. Numbers are a universal language, and computation and multiplication tables are more accessible to limited English speakers than are Ernest Hemingway or Langston Hughes.

Yet many students are proficient with arithmetic in their elementary years and then begin to fail when they enter the world of advanced mathematics. Algebra, geometry, and other areas become a mystery to kids who once called math their favorite subject. It is rare for students to sigh and say, "I used to be good at history." But it is all too common to hear students cry in frustration, "I was a really good math student, once!" Why does this happen?

Students today are so busy preparing for exams that they often do not have an actual understanding of numbers. As schools become more and more beholden to standardized testing, students are drilled to death with multiplication tables and math problems based solely on computation. Kids are taught "tricks" to help them compute. They have no idea what they are doing but can get the right answer. Their test scores are decent, and everyone is happy.

But this should not be our ultimate goal in teaching numbers. We want our children to understand the power of numbers, to appreciate that mathematics is both relevant to their lives and fun. Simply training kids to pass a test, like Pavlovian dogs, will only lead to the familiar story of students hating math when they reach high school.

I wrote earlier about fear, and surely a math class can be an especially frightening place. No one likes to look stupid, and the precision of numbers can humble anyone. I often warn young teachers that fear can permeate a math lesson faster than a session on any other subject. With history, if one of the kids gets an answer wrong, it is easy to spin his incorrect answer into something encouraging. If one of my students is asked his opinion of President Lincoln, and answers that Lincoln was a great pilot, I can rescue the child by commenting that in a way Lincoln *was* a pilot, steering our nation through a storm of trouble. But if a child says $2 + 2 = 5$, his peers know that the poor kid is simply wrong (unless we're reading George Orwell's *1984*). Math can be scary indeed.

Sadly, I have seen far too many elementary school math classes in which the teacher says the following:

Boys and girls, open your math books to page 142. There you will see five hundred multiplication problems. Please do the five hundred problems. When you have finished the problems, please turn to the back of your book, where on page 543A you will find five hundred *more* multiplication problems. Let's keep the room silent and do our math.

You've gotta love kids, because many of them will actually do all these problems without complaint. But here is my question: If a child can do ten multiplication problems, why make her do five hundred? And if she *can't* do ten multiplication problems, *why in the world make her do five hundred?* The only real purpose of this drill-and-kill strategy is to make life easier for the teacher. I have discovered more effective ways to spend a math period. No matter what skill I'm teaching, I value quality over quantity and give my students fewer problems than most teachers would. Since our entire period is not spent doing basic computation, we have time to do other things that help kids understand numbers and learn to love them. Here are three activities that can be applied in any classroom, at any dinner table, or during any car ride.

Buzz

The kids and I love to play a game called Buzz. It's a ten-minute math exercise with numerous variations that we usually play several times a week. All of the students stand, and I randomly choose a number—3, let's say—which I tell them may not be spoken aloud. Whenever the number 3 comes up in the course of the game, the word *buzz* must be said in its place. Then we go around the room counting to 100, with individual students announcing the next number. For example, if the buzz number is 3, the first student would say "One," the second "Two," the third "Buzz," and the next child "Four." I point to the child who is next to speak, and do not point to the kids in order. This way they all have to keep their heads in the game, so to speak, and concentrate on the upcoming numbers. In the current example, numbers such as 23 or 73 would have to be *buzz*ed because they contain the forbidden number 3. Students who get an answer wrong simply sit down, and we see who survives the game when we reach 100. The game in question would get particularly exciting when we arrived at the number 30 because it would be the start of ten *buzz*ed numbers in a row. The kids have to pay close attention; at the end of the series one of them would need to say the number 40 at the right time.

As kids grow, you can challenge them by adding new elements, such as multiples and fractions. For example, if the taboo number is 6, the kids might count in this manner:

1

2

3

4

5

Buzz (You cannot say the number 6.)

7

8

9

10

11

Buzz (You cannot say 12 because it is a multiple of 6.)

13

14

Buzz (You cannot say 15 because 1 + 5 = 6. Ouch!)

Buzz (You cannot say 16 because it contains 6.)

17

Buzz (18 is a multiple of 6.)

In still another version, students are not allowed to say prime numbers. It's fantastic to watch the wheels spin in a child's mind when her turn comes up. You can see her mentally running the rules of divisibility before she either says the number or *buzz*es it. Meanwhile, thirty-plus students wait silently. They respect the fact that she is concentrating. They've been there. When she finally announces "Ninety-one," I ask the class why she didn't *buzz* the number. Hearing all the children say that $13 \times 7 = 91$ is music to my ears. There is communal laughter and excitement and all kinds of learning that does not take place when doing a worksheet.

Marcy Cook

If you know who Marcy Cook is, then you already know she is a genius when it comes to helping students understand numbers. She is every bit as good as advertised.

Parents and teachers who are not familiar with her work would be wise to visit her Web site at www.marcycookmath.com. You will not be disappointed.

I met Marcy over twenty years ago at a staff development session, and she forever changed my approach to helping kids comprehend math. I use two of her innovations to make our math period more fun, fearless, and meaningful.

A Mental Math Warm-up

Many teachers admire the fact that in Room 56 we flow from subject to subject without wasted time. We always begin our math lessons with a mental exercise, and the transition to math from another subject is made infinitely smoother by using one of the great products that Marcy features on her Web site: "number tiles." Each number tile is a one-by-one-inch soft tile on which a digit from 1 to 9 is printed. A complete set of tiles from 0 to 9 costs a dollar. I long ago spent $35 to buy complete sets for all of my students, who keep the tiles in Ziploc bags in their desks.

As our grammar lesson winds down, I ask the students to put away their work and, in the same sentence, begin announcing a mental math problem. This captures the children's attention. While they listen to the problem, they quietly put away their grammar work and bring out their number tiles. The tiles are placed on their desks. The beauty of these mental warm-ups is that all the kids participate. When a problem is finished, they all hold up the tile they believe to be right. Since they are not called upon, no one is put in the spotlight and the fear of embarrassment disappears. By having all the kids hold up their answers, I can see immediately who understands the concepts and who needs help. This game can be played by kindergartners learning to count and trigonometry students searching for cosines.

Rafe: *Okay, kids, everyone think of the number 7.* (They do.)
Multiply by 4. (The kids silently are thinking of 28.)

> *Double that number* (56).
> *Subtract 50* (6).
> *Show me your answers.*

Immediately the students hold up their tile with the 6.

I love to weave other subjects into our mental math game. There are so many numbers we want our kids to know.

Rafe: *Start with the number of states in the United States of America* (50).
Add a dozen. (Now they are thinking 62.)
Subtract the number of Supreme Court justices. (The kids subtract 9 to get 53.)
Add the number of weeks in a fortnight. (There are 2— now the kids have 55.)
Divide by 11 and show me your answer.

All the students will hold up a 5. It is amazing how well the kids retain an astonishing amount of information.

Rafe: *Start with the number of pints in a gallon* (8).
Add the number of innings in a baseball game (17).
Multiply by the number of millimeters in a centimeter (170).
Subtract the total number of U.S. senators (70).
Subtract a half dozen (64).
Show me the square root.

Like lightning, the 8s appear.

By the end of the year, my students know their metrics, fractions, and all sorts of numbers that help us remember facts from science, history, and literature. This simple little game gets the kids warmed up, happy, and energized. By the time we are ready to focus on the skill of the day, all of them are ready to do good work.

I've seen teachers in upper grades use this game to reinforce geometry and trigonometry facts, the periodic table of elements, and important dates in U.S. history. It's simple to do, it takes practically no time, and the kids have a ball. Many students, in fact, like to run the game and make up their own problems for the class.

Marcy Cook Tile Problems

Marcy Cook has developed books and programs for every level of learning. She sells "task card packets" that include twenty unique problems. Each of the problems focuses on a particular skill and is solved by using the number tiles from the mental warm-up exercises.

The most basic task cards are designed to help very young students learn to count. These cards feature images of animals or objects next to a blank square on which the students place the correct number tile. All ten tiles are used once per card, so students can self-correct their work. If a child believes he can solve a problem with the number 3 but that number has already been used, he realizes a mistake has been made and moves the tile accordingly. There is nothing to cross out or erase.

More advanced task cards focus on arithmetic and other numerical skills. Each card teaches more than basic computation—Marcy's cards are special because they ask students to evaluate a series of tasks.

The sample card on page 70 features five problems. Remember that the student has ten tiles with him—one for each blank square. Look at the problem on the bottom left of the sample. It can be solved using the 4 and 3 because $4 \times 8 = 32$. However, it can also be solved with the 9 and 7 since $9 \times 8 = 72$. To discover where the tiles

Multi-Divvy Combo Tiles 1984

belong, the student has to solve all five problems simultaneously. The middle problem can be solved in a number of different ways because 0 divided by any number will equal 0. The student is forced to try many different combinations until he discovers the correct tile for each space. With practice, a student learns to analyze the entire card. An experienced and competent student will see immediately that the problem on the upper right can only be solved with a 1 and an 8. Although 0 × 8 = 0, this cannot be correct, because he has only one 0 tile to use.

Marcy Cook's programs offer a rich and complex alternative to drill-and-kill programs in which a student either knows an answer or does not. Her materials truly enrich the math hour. They help reinforce basic concepts to struggling students while challenging advanced students to stretch their minds. Many fifth-graders can add fractions, but can they use all ten of their number tiles to create three fractions that are the equivalent of ¼, ⅓, and ½? Marcy's tools reinforce that math is fun and that learning is never finished. My best students understand that mathematical excellence is earned through the *process* of learning—not by a test at the end of a chapter.

In addition, many of Marcy's programs involve multiple tasks and several sets of tiles. I often put three students to work on one problem involving thirty tiles, each to be used one time. Now the kids are not only working on numbers but learning how to cooperate as well. They improve their communication skills by learning the value of listening to one another. Suddenly, their work goes far beyond the world of numbers. The kids find themselves in a magical place where hard work, thought, and happiness converge to create the quality education we wish for all our kids.

Obviously, math problems and games are only a beginning. I will discuss more advanced thinking skills in a later chapter. But first things first: If kids are going to succeed in mathematics for many years, they have to develop a true love of numbers. As with reading, exceptional children find joy in numerology at all hours of the day. Math is not just something that happens at 9:30 in the morning from Monday to Friday but at any time and in any place.

Recently, the kids and I visited Chicago to perform Shakespeare for a business group. As is our tradition, the kids wanted to grab a meal at the Hard Rock Cafe. During a break in rehearsals we walked from our hotel through the snow and found the restaurant on Ontario Avenue. The kids love to look at the memorabilia, have a bite, and hope their teacher might spring for T-shirts. I was in the bathroom when the waiter approached the students. He saw the kids and ran back to get crayons and menus to color. When he returned, the kids giggled. They explained they did not need to be entertained while waiting for their meal. They were able to manage by themselves. By the time I got back, the kids were engaged in a rousing game of Buzz. My seat had been taken by the waiter, who was having even more fun than they were. He told me, "I wish someone had done this with me when I was in the fifth grade."

SIX

We Won't Get Fooled Again

My class performs well on standardized tests. Later in this chapter, I will share a few things I do to help my students prepare for such tests. But let's be clear about something: The testing obsession that has swept our nation's schools is detrimental to helping children reach their potential as students and human beings.

"This is your life on the line!" Mr. Intense is screaming at Lucy. "Your future depends on this! Sit down, shut up, and let's be serious!" Lucy is nine years old and about to take a state math test.

I witnessed this. Lucy later told me that what frightened her most was the fact that her teacher was so out of control, he was actually spitting at her.

Standardized testing has become a nightmare in our schools. Teachers have become so overwhelmed by testing demands that they no longer have enough time to teach their students the subjects they are supposed to master. Students have become so burnt-out taking the tests that they no longer care how well they score on them. Among the situation's many sad ironies, perhaps none is more profound than this: Despite the fact that standardized testing was conceived to help our children succeed, in practice it has only contributed to their failure.

I am not opposed to tests. We need to assess how the kids are doing. Accurate, fair, and reasonable examinations can help parents, teachers, and students see what skills are being mastered and what areas need strengthening. Having accurate data is a gift to all parties concerned.

But the current system of testing is broken. We are spending so much class time giving so many tests that the kids do not care anymore. The fact that they rarely see the results of their work only adds to their indifference. In April 2005, for example, my fifth-graders were given the *all-important, end-of-the-year, this-goes-on-your-record* Stanford 9 test from the state of California. The children did not get their results until October! They never get to go over their answers to learn what they did right or wrong. They get percentile numbers that mean nothing to them. It is ironic that the people most obsessed with testing children do such a poor job of creating conditions in which the kids will perform well. In fact, many respected educators speculate that testing companies do not care if the students perform poorly. These testing services have capitalized on failing schools and made a ton of money exploiting our fear of failure. Consider the following:

Every week, my ten- and eleven-year-old students take a test in spelling and vocabulary.

They take a weekly state-dictated math test.

They take three state-dictated science tests a year. That's four to six hours down the drain.

Many take English tests to prove to the district they are proficient in their new language.

They all take four district-sponsored literacy tests per year. These tests each take approximately ten hours of class time.

They take four district math tests every year. These tests consume between one and two hours each.

They write three essays for the district every year. Each essay
    can take up to *an entire day* to complete, and the chil-
    dren never see the results.

At the end of the year, the students spend *two weeks* taking
    the California State exams.

Allow me to do my best Edward R. Murrow impression: "These
are the facts." If you have come to the conclusion that our system of
testing is insane, imagine how our children feel. The fact that more
children are not running for their lives is a testament to their courage
and ability to hold their position even when the enemy has turned
their left flank.

Before I share some tips on helping our kids survive the war, let
me make one more point: *These "standardized" tests are anything but!*
At least once a year, newspapers print the results of "standardized"
tests to show us how schools are doing. School officials nervously
await the results. These test scores can play an important role in a
school's future. Failing schools can expect a loss of funding and/or
probationary status. But time-out. These test scores are not accurate.
They may highlight certain trends, but anybody on the front lines of
education would do well to look at the facts.

State tests are not proctored. They are usually administered without oversight—a teacher and a class alone in a room. Students tell
me about teachers who have stood behind them and subtly (by
coughing), or not so subtly (by poking or whispering), indicated that
certain answers were right or wrong. And on timed tests, some teachers simply give their students extra time.

When literacy coaches from our reading program meet with teachers before a reading exam, they do something so incredible it would
make someone fluent in Orwellian Newspeak stutter. They actually
hand out the reading tests to the teachers—a practice they call "previewing the test." Teachers read through the tests and write down

words their students will need to comprehend or define. Having seen the actual exam, teachers return to class, tell their students what is on the test, and then administer it several days later.

Miraculously, the kids do better on their tests! This allows literacy coaches to brag that their system is working. I know many teachers who refuse to take part in "previewing the test." But, incredible as it may seem, many teachers do take part. Apparently they have convinced themselves that telling their students the answers to a test before they administer it is acceptable. Let's get real. It's one thing to teach children to multiply and prepare them for an exam by announcing they will be tested on multiplication. It's another thing to tell kids to remember that there will be a test tomorrow and the answer to number 1 is 432.

How to Study

My students do well on tests even though they are not given the answers beforehand. We take testing very seriously—part of our philosophy is that anything worth doing is worth doing well. However, we do not spend enormous amounts of time preparing for specific tests. Instead, the students learn how to study *effectively*.

Many years ago I heard an interview with the Great One himself, hockey champ Wayne Gretzky, that had a profound influence on me. Gretzky spoke about his relationship with his father and, in particular, how his dad helped him develop his work ethic. When Gretzky was a child and would ask permission to go outside and skate, his father's "yes" was conditional. Gretzky was not allowed to simply go and skate around. He had to go to the pond and work on a specific move or shot. He learned at an early age to practice effectively and not waste time. It was a habit developed as a youngster that helped him become the greatest hockey player of all time.

The same is true with studying. I teach my students that *how* they study is far more important than *how much* they study. They learn that in order to study effectively they need to "create the conditions of the test."

The classic example of misused energy is the manner in which many diligent students study for a vocabulary test. They make flash cards. They write a word on one side, its definition on the other side, and test themselves when they have time. For some children, this seems to work. But I've encountered far more who do poorly on the test and moan, "But I studied!"

They did study, but not effectively. The test required them to write words and their definitions out on paper. Throwing flash cards did not create the conditions of the test. It's common sense, and our kids need all the common sense we can give to them.

Let's say the kids have a math test coming up. Before we head home for the night, we always take a moment to discuss the evening ahead of them and the manner in which they will study for the test. As I give very little homework, we usually have a conversation that sounds something like this:

Rafe:	*Okay, munchkins. You did a great job today. Who remembers what's happening tomorrow?*
Erick:	*We've got a math test.*
Rafe:	*Is that all?*
Erick:	*It's a test on integers.*
Rafe:	*And since you don't have any homework, you're done for the night, right?*
All:	*No!*
Rafe:	*Tell me how you're going to spend your evening. Are you going to look over your math book?*
All:	*No!*
Rafe:	*Why not?*

Soo:	*Because we won't be looking over the book tomorrow.*
Rafe:	*That's right. What is going to happen tomorrow?*
Soo:	*You're going to give us problems about integers, and we're going to write them down and solve them.*
Rafe:	*Exactly, Soo. Who can tell me some things you are going to do tonight?*
Edgar:	*I'm going to do page 265. It's a review of the entire chapter.*
Rafe:	*But we've already done that. It's not due.*
Edgar:	*I'm not doing it because it's due. I'm doing it because the problems are similar to the ones you'll give us tomorrow. I need to create the conditions of the test.*
Rafe:	*What music will you listen to while you do the problems?*
Edgar:	*None.*
Rafe:	*But Edgar, you love music!*
Edgar:	*I do, but there won't be music playing during the test tomorrow. I am going to do the work in the same environment as the test.*
Rafe:	*Jacob?*
Jacob:	*I'm doing page 262. It's the one with problems about subtracting integers. I missed some and need to practice.*
Stephanie:	*There are more of those in the practice workbook. You could do them.*
Rafe:	*That's true, you could. Valeria?*
Valeria:	*And you can make up your own problems.*
Rafe:	*What will you do tonight if you don't understand a problem? What will you do when that happens?*
Randy:	*We can call a friend.*
Rudy:	*We can call you.*
Jessica:	*We can come in early tomorrow and ask you for help then.*

Rafe:	*You certainly can. And I think you should stay up and study till midnight.*
All:	*No!!!*
Rafe:	(With mock shock) *Really? Why not?*
All:	*We need to go to bed early. Sleep is important. We'll do better on the test if we're feeling good.*

These are children who study effectively. In their quest to reach Level VI, they do work for themselves and no one else. They are prepared and relaxed. And they score well on tests.

Consequences

Parents and teachers can help their children by discussing the actual versus absurd consequences of doing poorly on a test. Of course it is good to teach young people that actions have consequences, but our national fixation on testing has become so intense that we often put ridiculous amounts of pressure on our kids. Not only does this make the children miserable, it diminishes the chances that they will perform at their best.

Some teachers tell students their futures depend on their test scores. Others remind the kids that poor performance makes the teacher look bad. In Room 56, I tell the kids a few things that help them relax and do better on tests.

First, I laugh with them at the whole testing situation and ask to hear horror stories about teachers who have gone ballistic on them after poor performances. This loosens them up. Then I explain an important concept: A test is like a thermometer. It's a measuring device, pure and simple. Instead of measuring temperature, it measures the understanding of a skill. I pose a question: If they do poorly on a math test, what is the actual consequence? Is their future over? Will the sun not rise the next day? Young people need to understand that a poor test grade is not the end of the world. Their parents will still love them, and so will I. If a student does poorly on a multiplication test, it means one thing and one thing only: He does not understand the skill yet. And I will be *happy* to show him again. Going back to the trust issue, I practice what I preach. The kids learn by my consistent actions that I will not give up on them or be upset over a test score. We adults must work hard to help the kids navigate the ridiculous hoops through which they are asked to jump.

Parents and teachers must also remember to *never* compare one student's test score to another's. Always measure a child's progress against her past performance. There will always be a better reader, mathematician, or baseball player. Our goal is to help each student become as special as she can be as an individual—not to be more special than the kid sitting next to her. As a teacher and parent, I always try to learn and improve, but I measure my success or failure against my own past actions, and never to those of the teacher down the hall or the parent down the block.

Test-Taking Skills

Many good teachers help their students learn the importance of becoming "test wise." This is especially crucial when taking multiple-choice tests. The SAT is probably the best example: Few would dispute that success depends just as much on test-taking skills as it does on intelligence. I use a couple of strategies to help my students perform better on multiple-choice exams.

In the same way that no one likes to feel stupid, everyone loves feeling smart. Each day during our math lessons, I engineer a moment that the kids love for just this reason. After our mental math games and perhaps a round of Buzz, we begin working on a particular type of problem for the period. Whether it is something as simple as addition or as complicated as algebra, I usually teach the skill and then give the kids ten or fifteen problems to try on their own. Let's say I'm teaching addition. Just before I give the kids their own problems, I put one more problem on the board:

$$
\begin{array}{r}
63 \\
+ 28 \\
\hline
\end{array}
$$

A.
B.
C.
D.

Rafe: *All right, everybody. Let's pretend this is a question on your Stanford 9 test, which as we all know will determine your future happiness, success, and the amount of money you will have in the bank.* (Giggling from the kids) *Who can tell me the answer?*

All: *91.*

Rafe: *Very good. Let's place that 91 by the letter C. Would someone like to tell me what will go by the letter A?*

Isel: *35.*

Rafe: *Fantastic! Why 35, Isel?*

Isel: *That's for the kid who subtracts instead of adds.*

Rafe: *Exactly. Who has a wrong answer for B?*

Kevin: *81. That's for the kid who forgets to carry the 1.*

Rafe: *Right again. Do I have a very sharp detective who can come up with an answer for D?*

Paul: *How about 811? That's for the kid who adds everything but doesn't carry anything.*

In Room 56, the kids come to learn that multiple-choice questions are carefully designed. It is rarely a matter of one correct answer and three randomly chosen incorrect ones. The people who create the questions are experts at anticipating where students will go wrong. When a kid makes a mistake somewhere in the course of doing a problem and then sees his (incorrect) answer listed as a potential solution, he assumes he must be correct. My kids love to play detective. They enjoy spotting—and sidestepping—potential traps.

When students in Room 56 take a multiple-choice math test with twenty problems, they see it as an eighty-problem test. Their job is to discover twenty correct answers and sixty incorrect ones. It is hysterical to listen to the sounds of the class when the students take a standardized math test. The most common sound is a quiet giggle of recognition. The kids love to outsmart the test and can't help laughing as they discover one trap after another.

The next strategy I use to help students improve their test-taking skills has to do with the way we correct practice exams. It is not enough to simply call out the answers and have the kids grade their work. We can't afford to miss a single opportunity to help a child get stronger—and correcting a test is as good an opportunity as any.

When we correct work in Room 56, no child is allowed to announce C if I ask what answer she got for number 17. The child must explain *why* she chose C. In addition, she must explain why she did not pick any of the other answers. In this way, students are forced to look, consider, and analyze all the options presented by the exam question. If we are grading a reading comprehension exercise, Peter must tell me he chose A because "in the second paragraph, on line 3, you can see the answer to the question." He must also explain why the other possible answers are wrong, and how they are carefully worded to trap the careless student.

We create the conditions of the test by grading a practice test orally, using the same thinking process the children will use when they are on their own. Students must constantly be pushed to exercise their critical thinking muscles. They must be asked to justify every answer they call out in class. By taking practice tests so seriously, the kids learn to attack real tests with the same amount of vigor. It becomes part of who they are, and the test-taking skills they develop will be useful to them for the rest of their lives. They consistently outdo other students who are just as smart as they are. Hamlet said it best: "The readiness is all."

The Heart of the Matter

How crazy has testing become? Many teachers from other schools visit Room 56 to train, and they are nice enough to keep in touch with me. Just this year an entire school of teachers trained in our classroom sent me Christmas cards—with copies of their students' test scores slipped inside, for God's sake! (Yes, that is a bad pun.) It is beyond belief.

I always remind my students that life's most important questions are never asked on standardized tests. No one asks them questions regarding character, honesty, morality, or generosity of spirit. In Room 56 these are the issues of true importance. Why have we lost sight of this? It's probably because raising scores a little higher is easy. Teaching honor and ethics is not nearly as simple a task. But if we want to create extraordinary students, we must be the ones to keep this in perspective.

When I am on the road with the Hobart Shakespeareans, not an hour goes by when we are not stopped by an admirer. Some of these people recognize us, and some do not. They have one thing in common. No one asks about test scores or grade point averages. They stop the children because the kids possess superior deportment. People notice their manners, listening skills, and a quiet respect for others that young people so often lack. It's wonderful that these students are good at taking tests, but even better is their sense of values—they know there are more important things than how they score on the SAT.

A few years ago, a letter appeared in the *Los Angeles Times* from a person who had witnessed something at the Shakespeare Festival in Ashland, Oregon. A garbage truck had overturned and the trash had spilled all over the street. This person was astonished to see a group of teenagers cross the street, pick up all the garbage, and help the driver get his truck in order. The writer of the letter was inspired to see young people who were so kind and thoughtful. Today, many of those same students attend Cal, Northwestern, and Notre Dame. They were able to get there because they studied hard in school, made sacrifices with time more ordinary students would not, and did very well on tests. One of them even made a perfect score on the SAT. But I am prouder of the day they helped a stranger pick up trash in Oregon. In an era when "You are your test score" has become accepted in too many school hallways, we adults must work hard to make sure kids know that their test scores are actually a very small part of who they are.

SEVEN

What a Wonderful World

Probably more than he knew, Sam Cooke and dozens of other singers crooned the absolute truth when they sang, "Don't know much about history . . ." The catchy pop lyric provides a dead-on description of how little our young people understand history and its importance in our daily lives. It is understandable given the current state of our schools. Consider the following:

- At many elementary schools, so much emphasis is placed on reading and math scores that teachers spend their entire day working on these subjects. In some classrooms, history is barely taught, if it is taught at all.
- The next time a school holiday comes up, approach any student and ask him why we celebrate the holiday. Odds are he will not be able to tell you the correct answer. Independence Day? Memorial Day? What does it say that the kids know nothing about these significant occasions? But here is an even better question: Can we honestly blame this ignorance on our students? In my elementary school, the teachers recently voted to cancel all Martin Luther King Jr. holiday activities—they took up too much time. Instead,

Dr. King is supposed to be taught as part of our "multicultural day" at the end of the year.

- No other subject is given short shrift as much as social studies. We have Black History Month. Does this mean African Americans do not have history the other eleven months of the year? Many years ago math teacher and part-time songwriter Tom Lehrer wrote a hilarious song making fun of National Brotherhood Week. His parody has become a sad reminder that when reflecting on the state of the union, most students today do not even know we *have* a union.

- As of this writing, our country has been engaged in a war in Iraq for three years. The other day I randomly stopped twenty-five seventh-graders at a school where I was leading a staff development session. I showed them a map of the world in which every country was labeled. You guessed it—none of them could find Iraq.

At the end of the year, all the students in Room 56 can label at least 150 countries on a blank map of the world. They can relate the history of the United States. They can sequence events from the Missouri Compromise to the Battle of Gettysburg to Watergate. They can differentiate between Theodore and Franklin Roosevelt. (Most students today have never heard of *either* Roosevelt!) Here are a few simple things I do in Room 56 to help my students master social studies.

Roam Around the World

In recent years the Internet has become a valuable resource for teaching geography. A number of Web sites feature excellent maps. My favorite is www.worldatlas.com. This simple site is comprised of outline maps of every part of the world. Each map can be printed. The site also features maps on which countries are numbered instead of labeled, with corresponding practice tests. Each day we spend ten or fifteen minutes utilizing the tools on worldatlas.com.

We spend varying amounts of time learning the different sections of the planet. It depends on the complexity of the region in question. South America is relatively easy. Africa and Asia are obviously more difficult. We may spend as little as a week on South America and as much as a month on Africa.

After the students have learned the countries of the world, and how to spell them correctly, we play a game called Table Points. The kids love it. They sit on top of their desks in tight groups of about six to eight. They do not have their maps in front of them. At first, I go around from table to table and ask simple questions that are worth one point: Name the state directly south of Oklahoma (Texas). Name five states that border the Pacific Ocean (Alaska, Washington, Oregon, California, and Hawaii). Name the two states that border Florida (Georgia and Alabama). When a question is asked, the students discuss the answer with one another before coming up with a group response. This fosters teamwork, listening skills, and compromise. By forcing the kids to visualize the world without a map, I help them begin to see our planet mentally rather than merely regurgitating countries on paper.

When a team makes it to twenty points, they get "bonus" money (to be discussed in chapter 11). One of the beauties of this little game is that when one team wins a bonus, the others still have a chance to do so. Each team that makes it to twenty collects its prize and begins again. The other teams continue to answer questions until they, too, have reached twenty. In this way, kids do not root against one another. Each team is simply trying to come up with the correct re-

sponse. Good answers are often applauded by opposing teams. Table Points are tallied through the entire year; the game continues forever, just like history.

Once the groups have each answered a few questions worth one point, the exercise becomes more challenging in two ways. First, the questions become more difficult: Name at least twelve states that border Canada. Name all six states that border Nebraska. Name the country west of Argentina. Remember, the students do not have a map in front of them. The second phase is to ask questions that, instead of being directed to a specific team, may be answered by any member of the class. These challenges are announced as "first hand up" questions. However, I add an important wrinkle to the problem. I explain that these are "four for seven" questions, meaning a team will get four points if one of their members comes up with the correct answer, but will *lose* seven points for a wrong guess. This forces the students to think before they speak. We have all seen kids who love to scream out answers both for attention and for their need to be first. Learning to think before they speak is a skill that serves students well in all areas of school and life.

The Extra Mile

It's true of all subjects, of course, but social studies can be especially boring or fascinating, depending on the teacher. Most history lessons begin with some sort of text, but it's impossible for even good texts to cover everything with the depth of relevance, excitement, and fun we want our students to feel when they study history. Good teachers and parents supplement history texts with additional materials.

Films, for instance, can be powerful tools in helping our students love and understand history. In Room 56, practically all holidays are introduced on the big screen. The films we watch together do not replace our daily lessons—they are shown after school and are intended to supplement the kids' knowledge of issues that have already been learned in class. As with audio books, showing a film is not an excuse to take a break. Days before the film will be shown, I begin building excitement by listing its title on a "Coming Attractions" board in our class. I prepare the kids by talking about sections of the film that may be difficult for them to understand. My excitement about the viewing transfers to the students. I have true believers before the DVD even begins.

Upper-grade teachers have more trouble showing films. There is not enough time during a class period to view a full-length film. Some teachers do a great job of using film to supplement their lessons during class time, but these sessions often suffer because the viewing is broken up over a number of days. I have a suggestion: Although it will not make your life easier, it's more effective to show films after school. This allows students to watch an entire movie in one sitting. It also allows for more discussion, both during and after the film.

Let me give an example of how I use film to supplement our regular lesson. Because I teach in a year-round school where classes begin in July, my students all get a Labor Day holiday. In general, students in the United States know next to nothing about Labor Day. If I wanted to be conservative, I would guess that 99 percent of the students in my school (and 99 percent of their parents, but that's another story) do not know why we celebrate the holiday. I think they should.

So, in addition to reading about the history of Labor Day and learning about unions, we watch all sorts of relevant films. Some we watch together after school, and some I simply make available to students for checkout. Martin Ritt's classic *Norma Rae,* John Sayles's *Matewan,* and of course Elia Kazan's masterpiece *On the Waterfront* are all films that get the kids thinking about labor—not only its historic significance but also its relevance to our lives today. If you want to go in another direction, showing Charlie Chaplin's *Modern Times* is a fabulous way to introduce kids to Chaplin's genius (most kids have no idea who he was) while also teaching them about the downside of the industrial revolution.

Labor Day is just one example. The judicious use of film to enrich history is a powerful way for students to learn about the past. *The Grapes of Wrath* is a must-see for students studying the Great Depression. *The Front* and the recently produced *Good Night, and Good Luck* are both excellent vehicles to supplement any unit on the McCarthy era. Many students these days have seen Steven Spielberg's extraordinary *Saving Private Ryan,* but a creative teacher might consider showing the 1946 film *The Best Years of Our Lives.* This film never fails to give students a powerful new understanding of veterans' issues.

Obviously, this is the tip of the iceberg. One danger here is the misuse of film. Unfortunately, many teachers show movies so they do not have to teach. Parents and teachers have to remember that, as with all things, they must set the tone and lead the way.

Documentary films also provide outstanding learning opportunities. The fifth-graders in Room 56 watch the entire Ken Burns masterpiece *The Civil War* each year during our study of the War Between the States. The kids not only learn enormous amounts of history, but the series also features terrific period music, which the students learn to play. In addition, the History Channel and A&E's *Biography* series offer seemingly endless good documentaries. I have copies of most of these films for the students to take home and watch. Presidents, inventors, explorers, and all sorts of fascinating people need to be made available to our students. Too often, students go home after school and waste hours watching awful television shows or mindlessly chatting online. Let's give them an opportunity to spend an hour with the Wright brothers or Martin Luther King. Such documentaries inspire, inform, and provide positive role models for our children.

Another fun way to make history come alive is to play historic speeches, many of which are available on CD or the Internet. If we are studying the Kennedy administration, it's easy to supplement any textbook by playing his famous inaugural address. I find the speech with a Google search and make copies for the kids. Hearing President Kennedy's voice makes his words so much more vital to the students; no text can match the real thing. From FDR to Dr. King to President Eisenhower's farewell address on the military-industrial complex to President Nixon's resignation, audio recordings provide a simple and fun way to enrich any study of the past.

I also use literature to help students learn about history. As an elementary-school teacher, I feel that it is essential to teach my students about Native Americans. Dee Brown's *Bury My Heart at Wounded Knee* offers a stirring introduction to the tragedy of the Indian Wars. But there are any number of excellent books, both nonfiction and historical fiction, that cover the Trail of Tears, Wounded Knee, and great chiefs such as Red Cloud and Crazy Horse.

Fine works of historical fiction exist for students at every level. It is our duty as teachers and parents to put books such as *Johnny Tremain, Across Five Aprils, Killer Angels,* and *The March* in the hands of curious young people. A passion for history must be nurtured, and we must take responsibility for sparking that passion by recommending books that are engaging and informative.

A Great Idea for Parents

Here's an idea for parents who like taking their kids on trips. Back in the 1980s, the National Park Service began publishing a little book called *Passport to Your National Parks.* When it comes to teaching history while you travel, I know of no better aid.

The slim volume costs around $10 and can be purchased at national parks and monuments. It can also be ordered by phone (877-NAT-PARK) or on the Internet (www.eparks.com). The book is divided into regional sections, each of which lists every national monument and park in that area of the United States. Kids can also buy special stamps that give brief descriptions of the parks and historic sites and are placed in a corresponding section of the book. Also, the ranger station at every national park offers a passportlike stamp that records the name of the place and the date of the visit in the kids' books.

Students of all ages love these books. My class constantly reads them when we are in planes or on the road. The books help the kids remember where they have been while also giving them ideas about other places they want to visit.

Each book contains pages for five years of travel. After my students graduate from Room 56, they continue to use their books to document trips to Frederick Douglass's home, Shiloh, Grand Teton National Park, or Promontory Point (the spot where the Golden Spike finished the continental railroad). Many former students grow up and buy these books for their own children. More than anything, *Passport to Your National Parks* helps teach kids that history is alive and ongoing—a never-ending exploration of the relationship connecting our past, present, and future.

Room 56's Favorite History Project

Each year as Room 56 finishes its study of the Revolutionary War, the students discover that Yorktown was not an end but merely a beginning. When the Founding Fathers met in Philadelphia in the summer of 1787 to reorganize the Articles of Confederation, they discarded them and created our Constitution. This revolutionary document must be studied by all truly educated students. People much wiser than I have predicted that thousands of years from now, the United States will be saluted by the world for three unique contributions: baseball, jazz, and our Constitution.

Back in 1976, the United States was celebrating its bicentennial. We honored our history with all sorts of events. One clever person came up with an idea that I use in Room 56 each year to help kids understand the Preamble to the Constitution. This person contacted the Department of Motor Vehicles in each state and the District of Columbia. He ordered fifty-one personalized license plates containing letters which, when the plates were arranged in alphabetical order by state, phonetically spelled out the Preamble to the Constitution. This incredibly creative piece of art was mounted in the Smithsonian Institution in Washington, D.C. If you go to www.allposters.com and look up "Preamble," you can order a poster of the display for about $10.

This poster hangs on a wall in Room 56. Each year the kids make their own license plates (insert clever prison jokes here). To make them we cut heavy construction paper into four-by-nine-inch rectangles. Then we use markers, colored pencils, and vinyl letters of different sizes to make the rectangles look just like the plates on the poster. Four kids might work on a California plate while another three work on Maine. It takes a few weeks to complete the project. By the end, the kids know all the states and their mottoes and have a full understanding of each phrase of the Preamble. "Promote the general welfare" and "establish justice" are expressions the kids take to heart. I have seen high school students skillfully make the same artwork out of various materials ranging from wood to metal. It's a can't-miss activity.

During a recent tour of Washington, D.C., the Hobart Shake-speareans were fortunate to have a fabulous group of students from Stanford University as guides. These young men and women attended the Stanford-in-Washington program and interned in all sorts of jobs around the nation's capital. Some of them worked for a California senator and invited the kids on a tour of the Capitol building. As the children toured the sites, the Stanford students were in a state of giddy surprise. They were mystified by my students' calm behavior and shocked to see fifth-graders identify scenes depicted in paintings and the frieze around the Capitol dome. The collegians remarked that many older, more "privileged" tourists had neither the deportment nor the knowledge of the young historians.

These children are not geniuses. They are ordinary, as is their teacher. They have *become* extraordinary by working hard and by being exposed to activities that go beyond the norm. As we entered the offices of the minority leader of the Senate, one of the children shocked the Stanford guides by noticing a painting on the wall. "Look," said Sol Ah, "there's Harry Truman." We need more ten-year-olds like this, especially if you consider that once we got back to the hotel this same little girl told me, "I was going to yell, 'Give 'em hell, Harry!' but I didn't want to disturb the senators." She's only ten, so who knows? Perhaps one day she'll be back in the Senate giving her fellow senators a little hell of her own!

EIGHT

Rocket Man

Teaching can be a humbling and frustrating experience. Even when things seem to be going well, someone or something will be there to remind you of your shortcomings. Unfortunately for me, one of the most painful (and important) lessons I ever received came from my own stepdaughter.

Caryn is beautiful and brilliant. She attended public schools and went on to graduate from the MD/PhD program at Johns Hopkins University. Today she works as an oncologist. Several years ago, she came to visit Room 56 for a day. Naturally, I was most excited for her to watch me teach a science lesson. Many elementary school teachers do not even attempt to teach this subject, so I proudly wanted to show my scientist daughter what I could do.

The kids opened their books and read about cells. The students paid attention even as they laughed at my bad jokes. Questions were answered correctly. The children learned about the parts of a cell and closed their books, ready for the next lesson. All of the students were orderly, polite, and involved. I was proud until Caryn gave my science lesson a one-sentence evaluation: "That may be the worst science lesson I have ever seen!"

Ouch! I picked myself off the floor and attempted to stutter a defense of my work. I told her I taught my class a daily science lesson.

Other teachers did not. My class finished the entire book during the year. Other classes left their books on the shelf, overwhelmed by all the time spent preparing for reading and math tests. Most important of all, I had students who openly proclaimed that they were going to be doctors and scientists one day, just like Caryn. At this point Caryn gave her evaluation an addendum: "Nope—it will never happen. No kid in here is going to be a doctor."

It shook me up. This was not some bureaucrat who didn't have a clue about teaching. This was a top scientist bluntly telling me that I was doing a poor job. (She was right on all counts. No student in that class grew up to be any sort of scientist.) Despite my bruised ego, I sat down and listened. She told me that to learn science, kids had to put down their books and pick up their equipment. They had to observe, experiment, record, and analyze. Above all, they had to fail and learn from their failures.

Now, years later, I have former students who *are* doctors. Several are environmental scientists. Today men and women of science write to tell me that their careers began in Room 56. Thanks to Caryn's blunt evaluation, I made some changes that have helped me help others lead exciting and meaningful lives devoted to scientific inquiry.

Please Touch!

The idea that a hands-on approach is essential to teaching science is nothing new. But how do we get there? Many elementary schools order science kits. Far too often, these kits are shared by various classrooms. They may be good for a while, but wear and tear usually ruins them within a year. Teachers often have books that direct them to perform various experiments, but what good are instructions if the items needed to execute them are AWOL? Most scientific endeavors rely on a control group, but teachers rarely have control of missing or misused resources.

Enter Delta Education, a New Hampshire–based company whose science products I have used for years. This is not to say that similar companies are not just as good—SK Science Kit, Educational Science Company, and the Delta partner FOSS all provide good products. I simply like Delta and have had good success with their materials.

Delta puts out a first-rate catalogue of science materials appropriate for elementary and middle schools. Their equipment is usually divided among life, earth, and physical science. They sell individual products such as microscopes or prisms. But the comprehensive "modules" were the items that caught my eye. These modules are complete science units in a box. There are different modules for every grade level, and the materials are always durable. Even if you do not consider yourself to be Mr. Wizard, you can teach fantastic science lessons using these kits.

Each unit contains the materials a class will need to perform twelve to fifteen experiments. In addition, a teacher's guide carefully walks the instructor through each lesson. If you can read and are willing to do the necessary preparation, you will discover yourself to be a far better science teacher than you ever thought possible. The teacher's guide simply and clearly gives the background for the activities, questions to ask the students, and a minute-by-minute guide to running the experiment. The kits even include record sheets on which the young scientists can chart their data.

The students conduct the experiments in small teams of four to six. In this way, they learn about skills that reach beyond the laboratory. They divide labor, plan, and summarize results together. Because teamwork is essential, these activities work beautifully not only in teaching science but in reinforcing the classroom culture I am trying to create.

The different modules cover dozens of subjects. My fifth-graders particularly enjoy units on chemistry, DNA, erosion, rocketry, and plant life. Each unit takes about a month to complete. For thirty to fifty minutes a day, Room 56 is a science lab—and the children love it. Many point to science as their favorite subject in school. Several have lamented previous classrooms in which their teacher "told us to open our books, played a cassette, and had us follow along while she went online to shop." Thank goodness my daughter gave me the kick in the pants I needed when I was drowning in a sea of mediocrity.

Finding the Money

Science is disappearing from elementary schools for a number of reasons, but one of them is no secret: a lack of money. All teachers use some portion of their meager paychecks to buy classroom supplies. It's ridiculous. And science materials are expensive. A good Delta kit might cost $300 or $400. It is unreasonable to expect even the most dedicated teacher to spend thousands of dollars for a year's supply of science materials. Let me offer one way out of this dilemma.

Every Christmas, teachers are showered with gifts from their students' families. Even in a poor school like mine, I see teachers carrying all sorts of packages to their cars on the day before winter break. As a male teacher, I could probably open a store selling wallets, ties, belts, socks, and mugs proclaiming "I love my teacher." This phenomenon led to an idea that helped me raise much-needed dollars for classroom supplies.

Early in the school year, when most classrooms open their doors to parents for conferences or some sort of Back-to-School Night, supportive parents will invariably say, "If there's anything I can do to help, please let me know." I came up with a good response to this generous offer. I inform the parents that I need science supplies and show them my wish list. If they were planning to buy me a holiday gift, I ask them to donate the money it would cost to a class fund instead. Parents, even those of limited means, are incredibly generous when they know their children will benefit.

Our wish list may comprise ten items with a total value of several thousand dollars. I never expect to buy all the items in one year. However, each year I am able to add inventory to our class science laboratory. As equipment is purchased, new items are added to the list.

In this way I was able to buy a Delta science unit. As the years went on I was able to purchase more. (Another good thing about the modules is that once they have been used, the materials can be refilled through Delta for only about $50.) Because the modules are used only by my class, they are kept in outstanding shape and can be reused over and over.

Let me offer a warning to young teachers: Raise this money quietly. While parents will love to help you, some administrator will always find a reason to kill the practice. He will come up with some sort of ridiculous rule. Make sure the parents know to keep their donations quiet. Most important, make sure to tell them in no uncertain terms that any donation to the class is completely *voluntary*. I have seen a few teachers get burned by not being clear enough about this.

I Don't Have Time to Teach Science

If you are an elementary-school teacher in your first or second year, you will probably find it impossible to teach science in the face of so many demands made on your time. With all the coaches, administrators, and pacing plans to contend with, it's no wonder you feel like throwing in the towel.

Do not feel guilty if you cannot get to science at the beginning of your career. Without question, you will need to spend a lot of time establishing your class culture and learning to effectively teach reading and math. Science takes a lot of planning. Even if a project requires only buying a container of salt, the ten-minute stop at the market may just be the straw that breaks your camel's back.

Take comfort in the knowledge that science will eventually be an important part of your day. As a new teacher, you will find that the majority of your morning will be spent teaching language arts and math. As you develop a rhythm, you will find time for a science lesson in the afternoon. I have seen some good young teachers alternate science units with social studies projects. The challenge for beginning teachers is to *remember* the value and excitement of science lessons, even if your school doesn't care if kids learn this subject, and to keep working toward the time when you can teach your students about science every day.

Because science is so expensive to teach, some young teachers try to build their programs a little bit every year. They use the school text as much as possible and supplement it with a Delta kit that supplies one month of experiments. The following year, the teacher may be able to afford a second kit, which leads to two months of experiments. With patience and planning, any young teacher might very well become known as the Pasteur of his school.

Failure Is Good!

A few years back a group of young teachers from a dynamic charter school was spending a day in Room 56. These instructors were terrific—energetic, bright, and caring. However, I noticed a key mistake in their approach to teaching. Their desire to help kids feel good

about themselves was so pronounced that they never allowed the students to get the wrong answer or take a fall.

We were building rockets that week. My students were working in groups of four. Each group was given a small Viking model rocket, instructions, and the materials with which to put it together. The challenge for each team was to precisely measure, plan, and assemble their project. One group was trying hard but making mistakes in the placement of missile sections. Several of the teachers kept going over to the kids to show them how to build the rocket correctly. On a number of occasions I had to politely but firmly ask the guests to leave the kids alone.

Guest: (Whispering) *You don't understand, Rafe. They're doing it wrong.*

Rafe: *I understand.*

Guest: *Their wings are crooked.*

Rafe: *Yes, they are.*

Guest: *The launch lug is glued too closely to the nose.*

Rafe: *That's true.*

Guest: *And you're just going to sit there?*

Rafe: *Yes, I am.*

Guest: *But their rocket won't fly!*

Rafe: *Not at first . . .*

Guest: *But . . .*

Rafe: *And then the group will have to figure out why their rocket won't fly. They'll have to come back to class and figure it out for themselves. It's what scientists do all the time.*

It's important to remember that we teachers individually define the word *failure*. In Room 56, a rocket that doesn't fly is not a failure. Failure happens only when students stop trying to solve a problem. It may be solved in five minutes, or it may take two months—as was the case when my students built an enormous roller coaster and could not create a loop with enough centripetal force to allow the cars to move along the track safely. But those two months of failed trials were some of the most fascinating and exciting times the kids had in science that year. And when the roller coaster finally worked, the kids could say they did it themselves. They understood the physics of the roller coaster. I did the best teaching during those two months when I decided to shut up and leave the kids alone.

Lab Rats

The biggest challenge to high school science teachers often springs from our embarrassingly shallow national values. In a society that celebrates people whose only claim to fame is plastic surgery or obnoxious behavior, it is a constant battle to show our students the beauty, glory, and deep satisfaction that can come from working in a laboratory. Today, most high school students are more concerned with what ring tone is on their cell phone than with working toward an AIDS vaccine or curing cancer.

Spencer Reams, a deservedly famous high school science teacher from Bellefontaine, Ohio, found the answers to these problems. Like so many good instructors, he knew his subject and taught it with passion. Unfortunately, his school was poor and lab equipment was scarce. Instead of giving up, though, Spencer worked his tail off for more than thirty years. He wrote grants, made connections, and created a magnificent laboratory in his school. Inside Spencer's lab, young scientists dedicated their time to astonishing work that few teachers would even dare to imagine. His students were more engrossed with DNA than with MTV.

Of course, like all extraordinary teachers, Spencer pushed the envelope. He kept his lab open until midnight over the protestations of administrators and fellow teachers. Students came from all over Ohio to do work there. Spencer was in the lab to hand out equipment and to guide his young people on their road to discovery, but he always let them choose their own paths. He left the kids alone. He let them fail. He did everything as well as a teacher could, but there was still one problem. Though he proudly applauded his young scientists' pursuit of excellence, other students were not so kind.

After all, we are the country that invented words like *nerd* and *geek*. We can't seem to leave kids alone who find physics more interesting than Paris Hilton. At Spencer's school, the students who diligently worked on their science projects were ridiculed by their peers. The phrase that took hold at the school was "lab rats." *Hey, look at the lab rats. There go the lab rats to their little cages.* I'm not sure I could handle such constant and cruel baiting even now, but I am certain it would have devastated me when I was sixteen years old.

Fortunately, Spencer is one of the great ones. He was too wise to take the bait. He didn't fight the taunts and abuse. He smiled and embraced them, and when he did, his young scholars found their courage. They accepted the label and even printed T-shirts for themselves. With a sort of "Yep, I'm a lab rat and proud of it" mentality, the scientists casually walked past the jocks and glamour queens daily (and nightly) to work on their experiments.

There will always be mean-spirited kids who like to insult young scientists with their calculators and petri dishes, but good science teachers will instill in their students an answer to the taunts. One of my former students, who is now an engineer at Berkeley, encountered similar problems when he was in high school. He would simply smile and continue with his buddies to the lab. From a distance behind him, he would hear the slings and arrows being thrown at him down the hall, but he'd keep walking. He often had a sly smile on his face as he thought to himself, *Hey, asshole, what's all the fuss? In a few more years you'll be working for us!*

NINE

Art Lover

I have no artistic ability. None. Any attempt to draw anything on the board—even a straight line—brings my students to their knees in hysterical bouts of teary-eyed laughter.

I am also the only teacher in history to receive the National Medal of Arts. Go figure. How in the world could that have happened?

When I was young and stupid, I entered my first classroom brimming with confidence and convinced I could change the world. I was more than a bit annoyed to learn that my young students had interests outside the walls of Room 56. There was an orchestra in our school, and the kids eagerly signed up to play. This meant they had to leave class twice a week for an hour during the morning math lesson. There was also a chorus, which meant another hour out of the room. I grudgingly allowed the kids to attend these music classes, while I mentally planned elaborate makeup sessions for the lost three hours.

I have to give myself a little credit—when I'm wrong, I don't go in for half measures. I was *completely* wrong to worry about these students. The orchestra was led by one of the finest instructors I have ever come to know, a woman named June Cheleden. She was able to manage more than a hundred students who had no previous musical training, and she had them playing difficult pieces within a year. In her spare time, she taught an orchestra at another school and found music scholarships and lessons for her more promising musicians. The kids adored her and couldn't wait to attend her classes.

Believe it or not, some teachers are so pathetic they actually discourage their students from taking extra art and music classes. I call these people "Copernicus teachers" because they substitute themselves in place of the sun as the center of the solar system. It's frightening to imagine the arrogance of anyone who thinks he is the only person who has something of value to share with students.

I wasn't *that* bad. I was foolish, though, to think that my music students would fall behind. I was shocked week after week: The kids in orchestra and chorus not only kept up with their colleagues, they did the best work in class. How was it possible? (Please stop snickering—I was green and very ignorant.)

I soon learned a basic truth about the arts: Students involved in arts education are learning about things far beyond the art they study. When a child goes off to play in an orchestra, he is not only learning to play the violin or clarinet, he is also learning about discipline, responsibility, teamwork, sacrifice, practice, correcting mistakes, listening, and time management. That's not a bad set of skills for a kid to have in his pocket. And to learn them and have fun at the same time is a pretty neat trick.

Once I saw the value of the arts, I became determined to work them into my class. It was marvelous that the kids had music lessons two or three times a week, but I wanted them to have more. The only thing standing in my way was my own limited knowledge of arts education. I began visiting every school I could find that was proud of its music, art, or drama programs. Before long I accumulated a number of great ideas that I incorporated into my classroom. Sadly, I've also witnessed some examples of how *not* to use the arts.

Caution: Let Them Play

Many years ago, I had a student named Joann. I have been a teacher now for a quarter of a century, and Joann is quite simply one of the most remarkable people I have ever met. She is brilliant, beautiful, and talented. She played several instruments, but piano and flute were her specialties. At the piano, Joann was a prodigy. Her wonderful parents found her the best teachers, and Joann spent thousands of hours honing her craft.

After elementary school, she won a scholarship to an elite middle school. One semester, the school put on a production of *Candide*. I love this show and, knowing this, Joann invited me to a performance. When I entered the auditorium, I saw Joann sitting at a magnificent piano. The thought of hearing this amazing kid play Bernstein's masterpiece thrilled me. I went over to say hello before the show, gave her a hug, and noticed the rest of the musicians. They were all adults. Joann explained that the school had hired a professional orchestra to make the show "better."

That wasn't the worst of it. Joann was a better musician than any of the adults, but she was allowed to play only the overture—an adult took over for the remaining two hours. Joann could have done this easily. The adult turned out to be the school music teacher, who simply wanted to perform in the show. Hello? So many schools have lost sight of who is supposed to be the center of attention.

Once or twice in a lifetime, we parents and teachers may find a brilliant artist under our tutelage. Most of us, however, even with talent and training, will never paint like Picasso, sing like Sarah Vaughan, or swing like Duke Ellington. Teachers and parents must remember that our children should be the performers, even if they are not perfect. That's the beauty of art—we strive for perfection but never achieve it. The journey is everything.

Too many of us lose sight of this fact. As a young educator, I made the stupid mistake of refusing to teach my students certain songs because they were "too difficult." In truth, the students' "inability" to play or sing something was simply a reflection of my own inadequacy. If I wanted the kids to perform better, I had to teach better. Once I understood this concept, and focused my energies on the children and the process of learning, I became a much better instructor.

In chapter 17, I give a detailed description of how Room 56 puts together a performance, but for now let me make a general suggestion: Whether your kids are giving an elaborate concert or putting on the tiniest of skits, we adults need to *get the hell out of their way*. I have sat through too many school shows in which teachers perform alongside their students because it's "cute"; I've seen too many adults take bows for helping with costumes; and I've definitely heard too many teachers play piano to accompany kids when one of the children could have done it. Sir Ian McKellen and Michael York, dear friends of mine, are two of the finest actors of our time. Yet they are never asked to play parts in our annual Shakespeare play. With apologies to Shakespeare, always remember the play's *not* the thing—the kids are.

Five Can't-Miss Art Projects

The creative journey does not have to take place as part of a performance. Works of art, and the benefits that come through their creation, can just as easily be accomplished on a canvas with paint or on paper with pencil.

Parents and teachers with real artistic ability may have an easy time teaching children to draw, paint, and sculpt, but if you're like me, classroom art can be a black hole of despair. I vividly recall the shame I felt in my early years when I watched students in other classes walk home with beautiful projects. I did my best to learn from the many good art teachers around me, but still I was art-challenged. To quote Bill Cosby, "Everything I began turned out to be an ashtray."

After countless failed attempts, I stumbled upon a few projects that have been wildly successful. These are certainly not the only fish in the sea, but here are some projects that my students love to create and keep forever.

Matisse Cutouts

Materials needed:
  Construction paper is okay
  Origami paper is better
  Photos of Matisse cutouts
  Scissors
  Glue or paste

It's always fun to introduce the kids to the life and work of a particular artist. My favorite artist to teach the kids about is probably Henri Matisse. His colors are magical, and I have discovered that students are captivated by his cutouts. They are always intrigued to learn that Matisse became disabled as he aged. Even when confined to a wheelchair and unable to paint, the artist had to keep creating. This is an important point to make to the students—that artists create because of the need to express themselves. A simple little thing like physical disability does not stop the human heart's need to speak. When he could no longer paint, Matisse thrilled the world with works of art made from spectacular paper shapes that he cut out and mounted.

A search of Amazon.com reveals at least half a dozen books with

instructions for Matisse cutout projects. I teach one such activity that begins with a nine-by-nine-inch piece of paper used as a background. The children then select a different colored paper and cut four squares, each four inches on a side. They have the choice of cutting four squares of the same color or four squares of different colors. In either case, all four squares are glued onto the larger background piece.

Finally, using other papers, the students cut out a shape; it can be any design, but they must cut four that are identical. Some kids cut out abstract shapes, and hearts, leaves, and stars are also quite popular, but anything goes. If the students have chosen the same color paper for their four-by-four-inch squares, the papers for the cutouts are all different colors. If the smaller squares are different colors, the cutouts are all the same color.

It's okay to use construction paper, but I have found that using origami paper makes these creations more vibrant. In any event, once the four squares are mounted, the kids will be fascinated to observe the optical illusions created by the different colors. Though the young artists know the shapes are all identical in size, their various colors alter the appearance. Thus, in this simple project, kids learn the effect of color, they learn about a great artist, and they learn that we do not create and explore the world of art for profit or fame. We create for the same reason we breathe—we need to.

Halloween Masks

Materials needed:
  Johnson & Johnson fast-setting plaster bandage rolls
  Scissors
  Bowls for water
  Vaseline
  Towels
  Acrylic paint

Every Halloween, my fifth-graders have a wonderful time making masks of their own faces. My wife, Barbara, goes to a medical supply store and buys Johnson & Johnson fast-setting plaster bandages, which are normally used for casting broken bones. The bandages come in different sizes and drying times. She gets three-inch rolls that dry in five minutes.

About a week before Halloween, I teach the kids how to do the project by demonstrating on a volunteer, who lies on a table that the other students gather around. The volunteer lies on his back while I walk the students through every step of the procedure, making sure to emphasize how important it is to be delicate when working near someone's face. The kids ooh and aah as the project takes shape, and a few days later they are ready to try it themselves.

The kids divide into groups of five. Each team takes a roll of bandage and cuts it into small strips, most about a half inch wide and two inches long. The class takes on the look of a M*A*S*H unit. One child from each team lies on his back on a couple of desks, a towel beneath his head to make him more comfortable. His teammates surround him. Two students on the team are the "doctors." They rub Vaseline all over the face of the "patient." They are handed bandages by their two assistants. Each bandage is dipped in a bowl of water on the table and applied to the patient's face. Slowly, all of his features are covered. We put on about three layers of bandages. Some children like having their noses covered (they can easily breathe through their mouths) and others do not.

The entire process takes about fifteen minutes. It is crucial that the patient's face be covered with Vaseline, particularly around the eyebrows and under the chin. As the face becomes enclosed, the assistants often cut smaller pieces of bandage that better match the bridge of the nose or the area around the mouth.

When the doctors are finished, the patient lies there for about five to seven minutes while the bandages harden. During this time, the team members help to clean up their area and begin cutting bandages for the next participant. Then it is time for the mask to be lifted off the student. It's gooey and lots of fun.

Each student writes her name on an index card and, in a separate area of the room, puts her mask atop it to dry. In a few days the masks will be as hard as rocks. Then they are painted with all sorts of colors and in all kinds of styles. A few days after painting, we apply the first of three coats of polyurethane.

Within a week, the kids take home gorgeous masks of themselves that are hung on the wall and kept forever. But that's not even the

best part about making masks with your class. As the students work
on the project, they learn to be incredibly delicate with one another.
If water leaks down a patient's face, one of the assistants carefully
dabs the wet ear or chin to make sure his peer is comfortable. Since
every child will eventually play every role within a group, the level of
empathy and teamwork is high. The kids are simultaneously creating, having fun, and practicing the kindness and caring I want to instill in all of them. October is a great month in our class.

David Hockney Self-Portraits

Materials needed:
   Glue sticks
   Camera
   Construction paper is okay

Watercolor paper is better
Poster boards or canvas boards are best

David Hockney is a popular modern artist who grew up in the United Kingdom but is based in California. He is famous for paintings and drawings of all kinds of subjects, from portraits of friends to swimming pools. He has also done pioneering work using the medium of photo collage.

Hockney takes thousands of photos of a single subject—a lonely highway, a room, a garden—from different perspectives over an extended period of time. He then overlaps the numerous photos and combines them to create one extraordinary scene. This allows the viewer to see a subject in a new and often profound way.

In Room 56 we use this technique to make self-portraits. Each child's face is photographed in six different conditions: one smiling, one serious, one plain, one silly, one looking to the right, and one looking left. The student then cuts up the photos—some kids cut them into one-inch squares, others cut them into rectangles or triangles—and assembles the pieces into a "complete" self-portrait. This one picture captures so many different moods and expressions. The students spend hours manipulating the pieces until they find the look they want. Some of the kids create outrageous, practically monstrous self-portraits that would be at home in a carnival fun house. Other students create serious self-portraits that tell their life stories far better than any single photo can. A little glue is applied and in a few days their "Hockneys" are complete.

This project is easy and a surefire success. The students love it because the method is fun and new to most of them. I love it because it stretches the kids' thinking and perception of themselves—and because it fills the room with laughter and easygoing conversation. God bless the arts.

Mondrian Magic

Materials needed:
  T-squares and rulers
  Canvas boards (frames are even better)
  Winsor & Newton acrylic primary colors and black
  Brushes
  Posters and photos of Mondrian art

When students study modern art, one of their first reactions is often, "What's the big deal about that? Anybody can paint a bunch of colored rectangles." I have found that the best way to disabuse students of this notion is to let them discover for themselves how mistaken they are. I start by introducing them to the work of Piet Mondrian.

Like so many famous artists, Mondrian's paintings cover a wide variety of subjects and styles. Yet he is best known for his examination of primary colors within perpendicular black lines. His paintings have become so well known that you see his work on clothing, purses, and T-shirts. When I first show samples of his geometric creations to my students, they remark, "They're nice, Rafe, but I can do that with a ruler and a crayon." I smile to myself. This is one of those "be careful what you wish for" moments!

Rather than hand out paints right away, I give the kids a day or two to create a few Mondrians of their own using paper, rulers, and colored pencils. Within a few minutes, the children learn two things. First, even coming up with a pattern is extremely difficult. Each time they think they've created a pattern with which they are satisfied, they begin to second-guess themselves (too much blue, not enough red). Second, the mechanics of drawing perpendicular lines of the same width is no picnic.

Days later, my previously cocky students are hunched over canvas boards with T-squares and pencils, meticulously drawing lines that will eventually be filled in with black paint. Once the lines are drawn, we use artists' tape to mask off the various squares. I used to make the mistake of painting the primary colors with cheap acrylic paints. Eventually I learned that it is better to spend some extra money at the art store and buy outstanding brands such as Winsor & Newton, whose colors are more vivid and alive.

The project the students believed they could create in fifteen minutes ends up taking weeks. But they enjoy every minute of it. Mondrian's work gives them a vision of what they want to make, yet that vision is only a starting point. The students delight in the process and do not worry about rushing to finish. They strive for perfection and focus their attention on each line, each right angle, and each brushstroke.

I cannot draw a thing. Yet with Mondrian as their guide, my students learn about patience, precision, the science of color, and the thrill of painting on canvas.

Beautiful String Art

Materials needed:

The Beautiful String Art Book by Raymond Gautard

Four 8' × 4' boards (¾" thick), cut into pieces 16" × 24" or 16" × 16"

Sandpaper

Flat wood exterior paint

Brushes

Wire nails (lots of them—about 400 per student)

Brass escutcheon nails (about 400 per student)

Hammers

Needle-nose pliers

Crochet thread (the more colors the better!)

This project is really tough, but what a project! It is for parents and teachers who want to go the extra mile. It takes vast amounts of time and patience but is a fabulous vehicle for guiding kids in the exact direction we hope they will go. In Room 56 it is the first project of the year, and it begins the first day of class. It came about years ago when I stumbled upon a book in the Los Angeles Central Library called *The Beautiful String Art Book*. The book, which is out of print but can be ordered from most online used-book retailers, features one hundred different string art projects. Even if most teachers are not crazy enough to try these projects with their students, parents can try them at home with children of all ages.

When new students enter the room on the first day of class, they see the wood flats already cut and stacked near the wall. They also see several spectacular string art projects—made by former students— on display around the room. Within a few minutes, the new students ask if they will be making them as well. "Not only are you making them," I tell them casually, "but you are starting them today." Without a lecture, the students have already learned something about the class: It's an exciting place and things happen immediately. In many classes, the kids sit the first day and have a teacher talk *at* them. Students are often told that certain subjects will not be taught because books and supplies have not arrived. In Room 56, we burn from the word *go*. It's an important point to get across to the kids.

During the morning, as the students work on math or geography, I pull a few of them aside at a time and show them the various possible designs, which include geometric shapes, animals, inanimate objects, and nature scenes. They choose one they like. Former students on summer break (I work in a year-round school and class begins in July) help out in Room 56 and advise the new kids on the block. These veterans know which projects are easier and which are more difficult—they help new students pick designs that will be challenging but not *too* challenging.

For the next several afternoons, the artists choose boards and begin sanding. We spend about an hour a day on this project for the entire first month of class. Having been told about consequences and trust, students understand that if they sand their boards carelessly or use materials improperly, they will not get in trouble—they simply will not be allowed to participate in the project. In over twenty years, I have never had to remove a student from the activity. They are too captivated by the completed projects on the wall to disrespect the way things are done in Room 56.

Kids begin to help one another sand. The former students work with the new students and talk to them about the year ahead. It's a wonderful orientation—the new kids learn about Room 56 from former students and work on their string art simultaneously. They all moan when it is time to stop sanding.

When the boards feel like silky marble, the students paint them. Each kid picks a color that will serve as a nice background for his string. I intentionally give out a limited supply of brushes. This forces students who have chosen the same background color to share brushes and paint. Within minutes, two or three kids are helping another student paint his board. When the recipient of the help is finished, he in turn helps someone else. The students learn quickly that teamwork creates friendships and leads to success with the project.

After a week, the boards are beautifully painted. I tell the kids on Friday that come Monday they will start working with their patterns. Hands go up.

Esther: *May I ask you a question, Rafe?*

Rafe: *Of course.*

Esther: *In the book, the string patterns are small. Our boards are much larger.*

Rafe: *Yes, they are.*

Esther: *How do we make the small patterns work on the big boards?*

Rafe: *You can't.*

Amy: *Then how does it work?*

Rafe: *I'm going to spend Saturday at Kinko's.* (The former students laugh.)

Helpers: *He lives at Kinko's. He's their best customer!*

Rafe: *They have a machine that enlarges the patterns to the size you need.*

Amy: *How long will that take?*

Rafe: *Four or five hours.* (The room grows silent.)

The message is received—the kids learn their teacher is willing to work hard for them. When they come to school on Monday and see their patterns all ready to go, the trust between us grows even stronger. *Our teacher does what he says he is going to do. We have to be the same way.*

I learn a lot about my students by watching them execute the next phase of the project. They carefully center the patterns on their boards and tape them down. While many string art patterns include dots to show where nails should go, ours do not. This is an added challenge. A student's instructions may note that sixty-one nails need to be evenly spaced around a certain circle or other shape. Because the patterns do not include dots, each student must use rulers, protractors, and all sorts of inventive methods to place hundreds of dots on the pattern before one nail is pounded in. Many children use string to measure the length of a curve and then straighten the string against a ruler to measure the total distance of the curve. Then they divide the distance into equal sections to figure out how much space should separate each nail.

It's fascinating to watch kids make mistakes. They use pencil and quickly learn that miscalculations can be erased and corrected. Before I discovered this project I never would have dreamed that art could teach children the beauty of catching an error, fixing it, and moving on. No wonder I'm an "art lover."

After days of plotting points, the kids are ready to nail. They will use from 250 to 1,000 nails per pattern, give or take a few. Again, I do not give each child a hammer. Two kids share a hammer and a pair of needle-nose pliers. One child holds a nail in place while the other hammers it home. This method of cooperation actually decreases the number of bruised thumbs and nails. The kids focus harder because they don't want to injure their partners. Perhaps more important, they get so caught up in the fun process of making the projects that they don't worry about rushing to finish them.

Finally, it's time to string the designs. Thanks to the instructions that go with each pattern, this is the easiest step of all. Most students start out using string of too many different colors and come to realize that less is often more—they usually end up going for simpler and more elegant looks.

A month of school has passed. The children have completed works of art that will hang on their walls for years to come. They have made friends. They have earned the trust of their teacher and their peers. They have planned, shown patience and perseverance, and striven for excellence. They have shared. They have succeeded. And I don't have to test them to see the results—their smiles tell me everything I need to know.

Consider yourself warned: This is only the beginning. Once you begin using the arts in your classroom, you will find them more addictive than chocolate. Whether you use music, performance, or visual art—or, better yet, all three—your students will grow in ways you never could have predicted. Your relationship with the kids will evolve into something strong and unbreakable. This bond will translate into students who are better behaved, harder working, and happier.

In a world in which everything is becoming standardized, the arts allow children to remain individuals—to march, in Thoreau's words, to a different drummer.

TEN

Put Me In, Coach

It's two-thirty on a Wednesday afternoon. At my elementary school, according to the schedule passed out by the administration, this is the period of time allotted for fifth-grade physical education. The playground has been reserved for the school's eight fifth-grade classrooms. Physical education is listed on the students' report cards as one of the skills we are supposed to teach and then assess. Teachers are also responsible for testing the students in running a mile and doing sit-ups, push-ups, and other tests of strength and endurance. These are national standards.

Our playground resembles a prison yard: It is surrounded by a sixteen-foot-tall chain-link fence, and every gate is padlocked. Yet it manages to contain four baseball diamonds, several handball courts, a painted circle that serves as a track, two basketball courts, and two volleyball courts without nets. There is plenty of room for the 240 or so students who by law are supposed to be out here staying fit and having fun.

But this day is like too many other days at so many schools: In addition to the kids from Room 56, only two other fifth-grade classes are outside. One is led by a good teacher who is running basketball drills with the students. They are organized and clearly working to improve their footwork. The other class is running all over a baseball diamond fighting for a ball as their teacher sits on a bench checking her watch and counting down to the three o'clock dismissal bell. The other classes are nowhere to be seen. They rarely, and in some cases never, go out for physical education. Some of these classes are led by teachers who simply do not take them. Others are being punished for poor classroom behavior. Some classes are not outside because *one* kid in the class misbehaved.

There is no upside to this empty playground. Our school's teachers are missing an opportunity to help kids become the kinds of students we love to teach.

In the first part of this book I discussed the necessity of creating a classroom culture that is conducive to teaching and learning. The playground, when used properly, can be just as effective as the classroom. These days it is all the more important to teach kids about the positive virtues of sports. In the span of a generation our culture has gone from celebrating athletes who embodied humanity's noblest virtues to celebrating athletes whose behavior on and off the court would land ordinary citizens in jail. It breaks my heart to see students proudly wearing the jerseys of athletes whose values are at best nonexistent and at worst deplorable. Fans and even sportswriters applaud players who admit to cheating and lying because "those things are part of the game." It is because of this disgusting trend, and not merely in spite of it, that we parents and teachers *must* expose our kids to the beauty of sport—and to the life lessons we learn from playing sports correctly and honorably.

Playing Correctly

The bad news is that most elementary-school teachers do not run effective physical education programs. Perhaps you see the importance of sports but do not feel competent to teach them. I have teacher friends who don't feel comfortable taking the kids outside because they did not play sports as children. The good news is that, as teachers, we can get better.

Some teachers take their kids outside and simply let them run around on the theory that it calms them down and helps them focus back in class. There may be some truth in that, but surely it's better for everyone if the kids can burn off energy while simultaneously learning a skill. Many other caring teachers structure organized activities—but without rhyme or reason. One day they run. One day they play kickball. The next day's activity is dodgeball. Imagine teaching math the same way: What teacher would teach multiplication on Monday, fractions on Tuesday, and integers on Wednesday? In teaching any subject, an instructor targets a particular skill and doesn't move on until the students have mastered it. Physical education should be no different.

Goals are a key element of all instruction. In Room 56, my goals for physical education are the following:

1. The students will have daily exercise.
2. The students will learn the importance of proper fundamentals.
3. The students will exhibit outstanding sportsmanship at all times.
4. The students will learn the value of teamwork.
5. The students will apply lessons they learn from sports in other areas of their lives.

Any physical activity can be used to accomplish these objectives. It could be hopscotch, volleyball, or basketball. As with all education, parents and classroom leaders should share their passions with children.

Baseball: The Most Sacred Game Ever Invented

I love most sports. I've played practically all of them, and I still watch them on TV and in person when I have time. I adore *fútbol* and follow the World Cup religiously, but my favorite sport of all is baseball.

To me, baseball is the perfect game. It's the only game in which the defense holds the ball. It's the fairest of all sports: One team cannot use the clock to prevent the other team from catching up, and even when you are winning, you have to give your opponent a chance to even the score. With its lineup and batting order, baseball is more democratic than other sports: Each player gets a turn, and a team can't keep feeding the ball to its best players. It is a game that has moments of stillness and sudden flashes of speed. To a casual observer, not much appears to be happening during a game. But a knowledgeable fan understands the game's intricate nuances, from the positioning of the defense to the batter's count.

In Room 56, we learn to play baseball. We spend the first six months on fundamentals and don't play an actual game until midway through the year. Month after month, the playground is simply an extension of the classroom. Even though we've moved outside, we are still guided by our classroom culture. Students pay attention. I teach. Each day we learn a skill and practice until we get it right. My lesson plan may reveal that during the math hour we are learning to measure angles with protractors, but it will also show that in the afternoon we are learning how to make the throw from third to first. Another day might find the students learning how to properly run the bases, turn a double play, or dare to attempt a suicide squeeze.

Initially many of the students are afraid to play, usually for one of two reasons. The first is that they are afraid of the ball. To avoid this problem, and because we play on an asphalt field without helmets or other safety equipment, we spend the first month of the year playing with tennis balls, which are lighter and softer. This allows the students to concentrate on learning the fundamentals rather than live in fear of being hit by the ball. We eventually switch to rubber balls known as RIF (reduced injury factor) balls, which can be found at any decent sporting goods store.

The second reason students are afraid is because of bad previous experiences. Young people rarely forget the anguish of being yelled at by a peer or parent for dropping a ball or making a mistake. In Room 56, we do not tease or ridicule people. This practice carries over into everything we do, including physical education. In fact, it is a *key* component of the physical education program in Room 56. Would students mock a classmate who couldn't do a math problem? Of course they wouldn't. The playground is no different. I teach the kids an essential truth of sports: When teammates make mistakes, they need our support, not our derision. I point out an irony of the all-too-common scenario in which teammates scream at the kid who dropped the ball: They are usually yelling because they desperately want to win, but humiliating a teammate only makes the "offender" more likely to make future mistakes—he will be playing scared. Students in Room 56 learn that being nice to a player who screws up (and who surely feels bad enough already) is not only the *right* thing to do, but the *smart* thing as well.

After about two months of baseball drills, we begin work on two other physical education units. I teach volleyball the same way as I teach baseball. Of course, it's the same way I teach reading or math. The volleyball players learn their positions. They are taught how to properly serve, dig, pass, set, and spike. Then they learn strategies and begin to understand how complex the game is, even if they once thought it was simple. We also begin running as part of our third unit of study. The goal is for each fifth-grader to run the mile easily by the end of the year. This prepares the students for the national test they will take.

Independent Practice

Now that the students have skills to practice, they are divided into three teams of ten or eleven players each. While one team runs the mile, the second team practices passing volleyballs. The third team takes batting practice with me. This rotating schedule accomplishes several objectives that make the kids not only better at sports but also better in the classroom.

In order to excel at anything, kids must learn to practice without a teacher constantly evaluating them. Sports drills provide a perfect opportunity for teachers to show kids they are trusted while also giving them time to do the solitary practice that leads to real improvement. Don't be afraid to let them practice on their own or in teams. One wonderful thing about sports is that they allow kids to compete against their own past performances. When a student shoots free throws or runs a mile, he can evaluate himself. If he can run a mile in eight minutes, his new goal should be 7:55. If a student can run only three-eighths of a mile, perhaps today he will try to run half a mile before slowing down to a walk. Always give students guidance, but remember that it's important for them to learn to practice for themselves and not for their teacher.

Keeping Statistics

In Room 56, the kids monitor their progress in sports by keeping statistics. In this way they learn to assess themselves and set goals while also practicing their math skills. No matter what sport or game they are playing, it's easy to keep records. If the kids are running the mile, have them keep a daily log of their times. If they are shagging fly balls, have them keep track of their success rates. The same goes for shooting free throws, practicing the long jump, bowling, or any other sport. Keeping stats provides students with goals and purpose—two things that will serve them well in all areas of life.

Even a simple game of catch can be recorded with statistics. When I first began teaching, I was shocked to discover how few children can actually throw and catch a baseball correctly. These skills may seem like second nature to adults, but learning them is not as easy as one might think. Students have to be in tune with one another, concentrate on the accuracy of their throws, and use their gloves correctly. In Room 56, we keep track of how many throws and catches a pair of students can make before the ball hits the ground. Each day the kids play catch, they are trying to set new personal bests.

The Ultimate Record Keeping:
World Series Night

When I was a kid, my father taught me how to score a baseball game. It's a difficult skill to teach but well worth the effort. In my early years as a teacher, I tried to show the students how to keep score in class before venturing out to Dodger Stadium to try it in real life. But I ran into problems. With thirty or forty kids spread out over three or more rows of seats, it was difficult to get to students who had questions. I didn't want to shout instructions or answers and risk disturbing other spectators. Finally, my wife and I solved the problem with an event that has become a yearly tradition in Room 56: World Series Night.

After spending several weeks learning to keep score, the kids stay after school one evening to watch a World Series game live on TV. It's the ultimate lesson in record keeping. I print score sheets for all the kids from the Internet, and they sit at their desks and score the game. As questions arise, I can easily maneuver around the room to help or write on the chalkboard. Everyone has a great time because in addition to keeping score, we eat hot dogs and Cracker Jacks and drink soda. After this experience, the kids are ready to try keeping score at a real ball game. One student's score sheet from a 2005 World Series game between the Houston Astros and Chicago White Sox is shown above.

After the game, the kids get down to math. They learn to apply their mathematical skills to real-life situations by computing batting averages, ERAs, slugging percentages, on-base percentages, and other statistics. Suddenly math and statistics are not merely subjects they learn in school, but tools that give them a better understanding of the game they've been playing outside. As a result, both math *and* baseball become more meaningful.

Going to the Games:
A Golden Chance to Teach

Many teachers take their students to sporting events. That's a good start, but I use such outings to do some of my best teaching. Whether you are a high school science teacher, a parent desperate to spend some time with your teenager, or an elementary-school teacher like me, a trip to a sporting event is a golden opportunity to teach kids not only about sports but about the more important, and largely ignored, issue of *sportsmanship.*

One of my primary goals in Room 56 is to teach my students to be kind in a world that is often anything but. Nowhere today is bad behavior more prevalent, or accepted, than in the sports arena. A trip to the old ball game offers a perfect object lesson in behavior that is boorish, obnoxious, and downright disgusting. At basketball games, for instance, fans scream obscenities at the opposing team and its fans. They think it's acceptable to upset the concentration of players shooting free throws by whistling and waving their arms behind the basket. To my mind, that's no different from tripping a player as he runs down the court. Today's fans believe they are part of the game. This mentality is now accepted even by people who are normally intelligent and reasonable. But it is not correct, and kids need to learn that fans are no more *in* a game than theatergoers are *in* a play.

I do use sporting events to teach my students that they are allowed to march to a different drummer, however. When the kids in Room 56 attend a contest of any kind, they usually root for a team.

They scream, cheer, and yell encouragement. They celebrate baskets, touchdowns, and goals. But they do not boo the other team. They cheer good plays on both sides of the ball. As athletes themselves, they appreciate outstanding performances by any player. They know what it is to both win and lose. They know that to participate in the detestable behavior exhibited by so many fans—to go along with the crowd—would be to make themselves the worst thing they could be: ordinary. They want to be special.

While it's sad that good sportsmanship is in short supply these days—both on the court and surrounding it—we must not give up on teaching it. We adults have to show the kids that for every drunken idiot screaming obscenities at the visitors' bench, other fans quietly acknowledge an opponent's good play with a soft "Wow" or "Unbelievable." For every headline-starved punk doing a touchdown dance on ESPN, there is an Arthur Ashe, Rafer Johnson, Chris Evert, or Sandy Koufax. These are special people, and our children need to be exposed to their greatness if they are to become special as well.

A few years ago, when our school actually had a physical education program, it held a volleyball tournament. Because of my students' disciplined practice and sound fundamentals, Room 56 destroyed every class it played, even classes made up of far better athletes. A teacher came up to me a day after her class was trounced by the Hobart Shakespeareans. One of her students had told her something that she found remarkable, and she wanted to share it with me. "We don't mind losing to Rafe's class," the child had said, "because they're so nice." The teacher told me she thought my students were something very special. She was right.

ELEVEN

Taxman

When I wrote *There Are No Shortcuts* in 2003, I included a chapter about the economic system used in Room 56. I have received enormous amounts of mail regarding this system. People love it, but certain questions keep coming my way. I hope this chapter gives teachers and parents a more complete view of how our economic system works.

In brief, for readers unfamiliar with Hobart Shakespearean economics, all children in Room 56 apply for a classroom job the first day of school. Students are given a list of job opportunities and descriptions of the work. There are janitors, bankers, ball monitors, office messengers, clerks, police officers, and other occupations. Each of these jobs differs slightly in pay. Janitors, who work daily, earn more money (simulated cash) than students whose jobs require their services only two or three times a week. Each child usually gets one of his first two choices.

With the job comes a monthly paycheck. The children deposit this with their banker. They need to save their money because all students pay rent to sit at their desks. The closer a child sits to the front of the room, the more expensive the seat. As I discussed in detail in *There Are No Shortcuts,* there are all sorts of ways to make extra money. If students do extra work or join the school orchestra, for in-

With a little help from a computer, Room 56 has its own legal tender!

stance, they are paid bonus money. However, if they fail to do work or are tardy, a police officer fines them. Students can use both class "checks" and "cash." Checks are practically obsolete these days, but I still teach the kids how to write them. At the end of the month, the entire class participates in a wild auction where school supplies and gift certificates are up for sale.

The kids love the economic system, as do their parents and other teachers who have tried it. For the sake of clarity, however, I wanted to explain the objectives behind the program. For instance, I have seen some teachers try to use the system as a mechanism to control their students, an interpretation that misses the point entirely. In *There Are No Shortcuts,* I focused on the *how* of the scheme; here I would like to examine the *why.*

Organization and Planning

I want to teach children real skills that will help them for the rest of their lives. Being organized is one such skill. It can be cute to hear a kid describe his room or desk as a nuclear war zone, but in reality it's a bad sign. Smarter people than I have observed that a person's room is representative of his state of mind. A child who knows how to organize and balance his time is more likely to find happiness by doing things he enjoys—and he's more likely to do them well. Learning to save money, balance a checkbook, and plan for future expenses takes organization. It's essential for young people to see the importance of orderliness and how to get there.

To get things started, I give each student a ledger sheet on the first day of school. You can buy pads of such sheets for a few dollars at any office supply store. I teach the students to label the top of the sheet with date, transaction, deposit, debit, and balance. The class usually employs about four bankers, each of whom supervises the accounts of about eight students. Bankers receive extra ledger sheets and keep duplicate records of their customers' transactions. In this way, if there is ever a discrepancy in the balance, the banker and customer can compare their ledgers to find the error. But the kids become so careful about keeping their financial records in order that this rarely happens.

A sample banking sheet from one of my fifth-graders appears on the next page. These records are the work of a ten-year-old kid for whom English is a second language. Because there is no father in her home and her mother works late, she often goes home to an empty house. Despite these disadvantages, this child is learning a valuable skill that will help her overcome her rocky start in life. Look at her figures—I know plenty of adults whose financial records pale in

Date	Transaction	Deposit	Debit			Balance
7/21	Bonus Money	2050				2050
7/29	Pay Check	700				2750
7/29	Bonus Money	1050				3800
8/01	Bonus Money	400				4200
8/01	July Condo		4200			0
9/02	Bonus Money	1350				1350
9/07	August Pay Check	2550				3900
9/08	Buying Eliza's Seat		3450			450
9/12	Bonus Money	1900				2350
9/19	Bonus Money	1100				3450
10/03	Eliza's Rent	1400				4850
10/03	Bonus Money	1500				6350
10/10	Bonus Money	1200				7550
10/10	Bonus Money	300				7850
10/19	Bonus Money	1750				9600
10/20	Bonus Money	1400				11000
10/20	Bonus Money	300				11300
10/21	Bonus Money	300				11600
10/26	Bonus Money	1600				13200
10/2?	Eliza's Rent	1500				14700
11/21	Bonus Money	5900				20600
12/07	Bonus Money	1150				21750
1/05	Eliza's Rent	1600				23350
1/05	Bonus Money	1300				24650
1/18	Bonus Money	800				25450
1/23	Bonus Money	650				26100
1/29	Bonus Money	2700				28800
2/02	Eliza's Rent	1650				30450
2/03	Bonus Money	3800				34250
3/02	Eliza's Rent & Bonus Money	3900				38150
3/06	Buy Science Chemistry		14000			24150
3/27	Bonus Money	1000				25150
3/30	Pay Check	3550				28700
3/30	Eliza's Rent	1800				30500

comparison. It is no surprise that her desk is immaculate as well. She is careful with her time, making sure to finish her homework before practicing guitar and violin. Her weekends are spent playing with friends because her work has been finished. She manages her time well because she is organized. Her ledger sheets and banking records are emblematic of her lifestyle.

Ownership

Students have to pay rent each month to sit at their desks. However, if a child can save up triple his rent, he is allowed to purchase his seat and call it a condominium. Some kids even carefully save enough money to buy the seats of other students and charge them rent every month!

As the clever students buy up property, they begin to understand the value of ownership. Each month they see their peers scramble to pay the rent while their own bank accounts bulge. They begin to empathize with the plight of their parents. The property owners in Room 56 discover that owning their own homes leaves them with disposable income to spend on exciting treasures at the monthly auction. As the months fly by, they learn through firsthand experience the benefits of saving money and owning property. The students who continue to pay rent learn the same lessons—and probably with more poignancy.

The goal is not to create a real-life Monopoly game in the classroom, but rather to expose the students to the benefits of ownership. The sad reality is that not one student in Room 56 lives in a family-owned home; all of them come from families that pay rent. One day, I want each of them to own his or her own house.

One of the most gratifying parts of my job is hearing from former students who have gone on to become very successful. Most of them buy their own homes, and a surprising number have even bought homes for their parents. I can't take any credit for this phenomenon, but it makes my heart light to think that Room 56's economic system might have played some tiny role in helping them appreciate the benefits of ownership.

A Penny Saved

If you've ever been on the road with your own children or a student group, you've probably noticed something: Kids are downright terrible with money. If they have five dollars in their pocket, they'll spend it. They'll buy anything. To paraphrase George Carlin, they'll buy a left-nostril inhaler with the words *New York City* engraved on it. Kids return from trips with their pockets empty.

I want to teach my students the value of thrift. It's not listed as a California State Standard, but being careful with money is a valuable lesson to learn. If you ever take a tour of Monticello, Thomas Jefferson's home, the docent will describe our third president as the Master of Time and Space. He did not waste either of them. Yet two hundred years later we've become a wasteful society. For example, at our school the students receive free breakfast and lunch. Yet much of that free food winds up in the garbage cans, discarded by children who do not consider the sad meaning of their actions.

Through economics, the kids learn both to be thrifty with their money and to value their belongings. When a student has to work to buy a book or calculator, he takes better care of it. Don't get me wrong: I am not a materialist and am far from cheap. In Room 56 we use the best instruments, the most expensive baseball gloves, and art supplies that are, well, state of the art. We like good things, and because the kids have to work and sacrifice to earn them, they appreciate their belongings.

By participating in auctions at the end of the month, the students learn to spend their money wisely. There may be an item for sale that excites them. Perhaps it's a complete set of *The Chronicles of Narnia* or a gift certificate to Barnes & Noble. Hands shoot into the air and the kids begin calling out offers. Often a student gets so caught up in the competition that he winds up emptying his bank account for an item he doesn't really care about. When the excitement of the auction fades, he looks at his prize and asks himself, *Was it worth it?* This is a good question for our future consumers to ask themselves when they are young. Many students learn the hard way that it's rarely a good idea to empty their bank accounts in highly emotional situations; something better might come up for sale just around the corner.

This system teaches kids to save. I see it when we are on the road. They do not buy very much. They are unimpressed with slick advertising or enticing displays. This is a virtue that serves them well in college and beyond. We all have to learn to live on a budget at some point, and it can't hurt to start when we're little kids.

Delayed Gratification

By helping the kids learn to save money, the economic system teaches another important principle: delayed gratification. In our fast-food society, young people are encouraged to want everything and to want it *now.* But Room 56's program teaches students that those who save money and spend prudently almost always wind up in better financial situations than those who spend recklessly in pursuit of immediate satisfaction.

Take a student like Amy. She didn't make a fuss about it, but early in the year she decided to sit quietly and refrain from bidding in the auctions. She was the student who inconspicuously did extra work, joined every optional activity, and studied tirelessly to earn top grades. You guessed it: Partway through the year, Amy snapped up several pieces of property. She ended the school year with the most desirable auction items—all because she understood that the best things come to those who wait.

The kids in Room 56 take this lesson and apply it to their quest to be the first person in their family to attend college. In high school, while some students waste time and blow off studying, these kids apply themselves seriously. They have fun, but it's balanced with an understanding that by working hard today they are opening a door to a much better tomorrow. They delay their gratification. They may not be the most popular kids in class, and they certainly aren't the most visible—that is, until senior year. It's amazing how people tend to notice the kids who get the scholarships to the top colleges. Recently, a former student named Linda e-mailed me about a "problem" she had—she was accepted by so many colleges she was having difficulty making a final decision. She remained humble, but confided to me that when peers marveled at her "luck," she would think to herself that luck had very little to do with her good fortune—it was mostly hard work and perseverance.

A Skill for a Lifetime

Several years ago I knew a teacher who was one of the most popular leaders in our school. When her students would talk to me, the conversation usually went something like this:

Christine: *One day I'm going to be in your class.*
Rafe: *Great! Who's your teacher now?*
Christine: *Miss Popular.*
Rafe: *Fantastic! Do you enjoy your class?*
Christine: *I love Miss Popular. She's the best!*
Rafe: *She is? Cool! Why is she the best?*
Christine: *She's the best!*
Rafe: *Got it. Why is that?*
Christine: *'Cause she's the best!*
Rafe: *Yes, you've mentioned that. Tell me something you've learned from her.*
Christine: *Well . . . umm . . .*
Rafe: *Oh, come on. What have you learned in class this year?*
Christine: (Forehead wrinkled with concentration) *We learned poetry!*
Rafe: *Terrific! Can you recite a poem for me?*
Christine: *Uh, well, no, not exactly.*

Rafe: *Can you tell me a poem you read?*
Christine: *I kinda forgot them . . .*

Clearly such a teacher *isn't* the best. But the kids loved her. She was one of those teachers who thought it was cute to get nine-year-olds to act like teenagers. She would invite them to sleepovers at her house and have dance parties and games far too mature for small children. Still, her legacy will be that she was the best.

But I beg to differ. To help young people become remarkable, we need to challenge them with lessons they will use for the rest of their lives. The Hobart Shakespearean economic system does just that. Last year I received a letter from Helen, a former student who attends Washington and Lee University in Virginia. During her third year of college, she chose to study abroad. She wrote me a letter and mentioned something that is a more accurate measure of classroom success than any standardized test. Living with other students in Japan, she remarked that all of her friends were having financial troubles and had desperately wired their parents for more money. Helen told me she was the only one in good shape. With her appreciation of thrift, sticking to a budget, and delaying gratification, Helen not only had enough money to survive, but planned to travel to other countries before returning to the States. And she was a poor kid. She thanked me and wrote that unlike the other students, she had a complete understanding of economic responsibility. She had learned it in the fifth grade.

PART THREE

THE MADNESS

—————wwwwwwwww—————

Damn the Torpedoes!

Full Speed Ahead!

TWELVE

Think for Yourself

Proceed at your own risk. This is a chapter for teachers who are insanely dedicated but still want to do more. If you think Don Quixote had the right idea, go ahead and keep reading. If you love teaching so much that you would do it for free, roll up your sleeves. If your highest high is watching young people achieve things they didn't even know were possible, you've come to the right place.

Every morning for the last twenty-odd years, Room 56 has opened for business at 6:30 A.M. I arrive at school in total darkness, well over an hour before classes begin, and find eager students waiting to get to work. These students are here voluntarily, and together we spend more than an hour working on a skill that is too often overlooked: problem solving. I'm the first to admit that I've made countless mistakes in my career, and I'm constantly making corrections and improvements, but the idea of starting the school day early to work on problem solving is one I've never regretted and never will. Like many great ideas, it began by accident—in this case, as a misguided quest to win a contest. But it has evolved into one of the most valuable hours of my students' day.

Today the kids in Room 56 are terrific problem solvers, but this wasn't always the case. Early in my career I taught analytical thinking and problem solving because I wanted my kids to win math competitions that were periodically held at my school. The winning classes went on to compete against other schools and districts. My students were successful in these contests, and I was foolish enough to be proud of this. It took me far too long to realize that by focusing on winning contests, I was missing important opportunities to teach lessons of real and lasting value. The purpose of teaching problem solving should be to develop the *process* of thinking and analyzing. This will help young people solve problems in math class and in their everyday lives. To hope to win a contest is Level II thinking. I wanted to aim higher, and I wanted to take the students with me.

As I am not a particularly creative teacher, I decided to give the kids the most valuable thing I have to offer: my time. I spend an enormous amount of time with my students. I work with them practically every day of vacation. We work on Saturdays. During the week we sometimes remain in class until dinnertime.

I am no saint. I often wish I were on a tennis court or at a concert with my wife. That's the price I pay. But the cost is far outweighed by the payoff: Some of the best learning in Room 56 takes place during unofficial hours, before and after school. Every kid in the room during those times is present because he wants to be. There are never discipline problems. All I have to do is teach, and that is a joy. It's rather poetic that our problem-solving sessions start in the dark and end with the coming of light as the sun rises and regular school begins.

The Bible

At the beginning of the year, I play a little game with the students. I tell them we are going to solve some difficult problems. I ask them to show me that they are ready to do so. Almost all of them demonstrate their readiness by taking out some paper and picking up a pencil.

I start laughing. I ask the kids why they are holding pencils. The first lesson is that pencils do not solve problems—people do. The kids learn that the first step in solving a problem is to put down their pencils and understand the challenge in front of them. At this point I hand out copies of "the Bible." In Room 56, this is not the New or Old Testament, but a sheet of paper the kids are given the first day of problem-solving class. It is taped to their desks and recited (forgive me) religiously. There are many variations of such a sheet, but ours looks like this:

HOW TO SOLVE A PROBLEM

Step I. Understand the Problem
(Put your pencil down)

Collect Relevant Data

Step II. Choose an Appropriate Strategy

Act It Out
Choose an Operation
Draw a Picture
Guess and Check
Look for a Pattern
Make a Chart or Table
Make an Organized List
Use Logical Reasoning
Work Backwards

Step III. Solve the Problem
(Pick your pencil up)

Step IV. Analyze

Does My Answer Make Sense?

The kids and I go over these problem-solving steps until they are sick of repeating them. My eyes were first opened to the importance of teaching the process of thinking by an inspiring math teacher named Randy Charles. He identified two expressions that frustrated teachers constantly use in the classroom: "Use your head" and "Read it again."

When a student is having trouble with a problem, his teacher will sometimes lose patience and bark, "Use your head!" Use your head? What in the world does that mean? I have never seen anyone get results by using this command. Then there is "Read it again." This phrase usually comes out when a student has mustered up the courage to ask his teacher for help on a problem. When the intimidated child is ordered to "read it again," he is usually too afraid to answer, "Look, lady, I've read it twelve times and I still don't get it. I need some help, dammit!"

We parents and teachers must do better than trotting out meaningless directions for our struggling children. The Bible gives my students an actual road map of the problem-solving process. It shows them how to understand, attack, and solve a problem.

Early in the year, the students are divided into groups of four. I tell them that we are going to spend a week practicing each strategy in the Bible. We might spend the first week learning to solve problems by drawing pictures. In that case I would start by giving the students a simple problem such as this:

> John has baked a rectangular birthday cake for his friend's birthday. He places the candles two inches apart all around the cake. There are six candles on each long side and five candles on each short side. How long is the cake? How wide is the cake? How many candles are on the cake?

Students who lack experience solving problems would not be able to come up with any sort of answer to this question. Other students, typically those who learn how to compute but haven't learned analytical skills, might answer that the cake contains 22 candles (6 + 6 + 5 + 5). They will calculate that the cake is 12 inches long (6 × 2) and 10 inches wide (5 × 2). They will write down their answer and move on to other problems. Unfortunately, this answer is wrong.

Here is a typical session with the students early in their training in problem solving. It's about 6:40 A.M. when the kids have finished reading the problem. The kids are sitting up and their pencils are down.

Rafe:	*What is the first thing we need to do to solve this? What is Step I?*
All:	*Understand the problem.*
Rafe:	*How do we do that?*
Jessica:	*Collect relevant data.*
Rafe:	*What does relevant mean?*
All:	*Important.*
Rafe:	*What is data?*
Kyu:	*Information.*
Rafe:	*When we read problems, is data always relevant?*
All:	*No!*
Rafe:	*That's right. Sometimes data is irrelevant. Who can give me some relevant data?*
Lucy:	*A cake is being baked. It's a rectangle.*
John:	*There are six candles on the long side.*
Rafe:	*How many long sides will there be?* (Checking for understanding)
All:	*Two!*
Stephanie:	*There are five candles on the short side.*
Rafe:	*Anything else?*
Class:	(silence)
Rafe:	*Well, how far apart does John place the candles?* (Guiding students to an understanding of the data)

Edgar:	*Two inches.*
Rafe:	*That's right, Edgar. I think we have our data and understand the problem. Who can tell me what Step II is?*
All:	*Choose an appropriate strategy.*
Rafe:	*Thank you for remembering to use the word* appropriate. *Does anyone think they know what the appropriate strategy would be?*
Sol Ah:	*Draw a picture.*
Rafe:	*That's right.* (The students know we are working on "draw a picture" problems.) *So it's time for Step III. What is Step III?*
All:	*Pick up our pencils and solve the problem.*
Rafe:	*And then we're done.*
All:	*No! We need to analyze.*
Rafe:	*So let's go to work.*

The kids work in groups of four and begin drawing pictures. They soon realize that the candles in the corners of the cake count toward the number of candles on both the long and short sides. The students will discover that the cake holds only eighteen candles. They learn that the answer to a problem becomes obvious when they choose an appropriate strategy—in this case, drawing a picture.

By working in groups of four and coming up with one answer, the students do more than solve the problem. Ideas are shared. Friendships are formed. The kids learn to listen to one another. They also, to quote Dr. King, learn to disagree without becoming disagreeable. When students come up with conflicting answers, they do not argue. Instead, each problem solver gets his turn within the group to explain his thinking. It is fascinating to see how many students discover their mistakes by listening to their own incorrect solutions.

As the weeks turn into months, these early birds solve hundreds of word problems. After a while, I no longer lead them through the steps. Instead, the students are given a sheet of problems, and the groups themselves decide on appropriate strategies. Many math teachers encourage students to solve problems by looking for "key words." The focus is on getting the right answer. The kids in Room 56 also want to get the correct answer, but they understand that the *process* of discovering the correct answer is more important than the answer itself.

Here are typical problems the students are asked to solve:

1. QUESTION

Moises saw a group of birds. One-half of the group was parakeets. One-quarter of the group was eagles. The rest were geese. There were 3 geese. How many of the birds were eagles?

ANSWER

There were 3 eagles.

Students need to recognize the appropriate strategy here is to *choose an operation.* This means that addition, subtraction, multiplication, or division will lead to the correct answer. In this problem, students need to add ½ + ¼ and subtract the total from the whole (1 − ¾) to discover that the "rest were geese" amount must be ¼. Since there were 3 geese, and these geese represent ¼ of the birds, the eagles represent the same number. Some students who struggle to understand fractions may find *draw a picture* a helpful strategy. This helps students see that there might be more than one way to think, another benefit to working on solving problems.

2. QUESTION

Three waitresses—Dulce, Marilyn, and Tracy—put all their tips in one jar. Dulce went home first and took one-third of the money as her share. Marilyn, not knowing Dulce had taken her share, took what she thought was her share. Tracy, unaware that the others had already taken what they thought were their shares, took one-third of the remaining money and left $8 in the jar. How much money was in the tip jar in the beginning?

ANSWER

There was $27 in the tip jar in the beginning.

Students will recognize that this is a *working backwards* problem. Since the last waitress, Tracy, left $8 in the jar, she took $4, the share she believed to be correct. That means there was $12 in the jar before she took any money. This $12 was left by Marilyn, the second waitress. The same reasoning means Dulce left $18 behind. It also means Dulce took $9, indicating there was a total of $27 at the beginning.

3. QUESTION

At the Hobart Shakespearean math contest, each student was given 20 problems. Five points were awarded for each correct answer, and 2 points were deducted for each incorrect answer. Elena's score was 72. How many correct answers did she have?

ANSWER

Elena had 16 correct answers.

While older students would use algebra to find this answer, younger students can *guess and check.* Knowing there were 20 problems given, a student can guess how many were correct. If the initial guess is, say, 14, this guess can be checked with computation. Fourteen correct answers would earn 70 points, but the 6 incorrect answers would give Elena a total of 58. The student sees her guess of 14 was too low, so another guess is made. This strategy helps students estimate, evaluate, and strengthen their reasoning.

4. QUESTION

At the end of the summer, Sir Ian McKellen wanted to give some gifts to the Hobart Shakespeareans. He made up a game to see who would get gifts. He lined up the children and found he had 100. He gave the first child 100 sticks. He asked him to keep one and then walk down the line and give each child a stick. After doing his duty, the first child returned to the line, never to be called on again. Then Sir Ian told the second child to walk down the line and take a stick from each even-numbered child starting with himself. The third child walked down the line looking only at children who were multiples of 3 and did two things. He took a stick from any child who had one, and he gave a stick to any who didn't. The fourth child did the same thing with children who were multiples of 4, and this continued all the way to the hundredth child. The game continued in this way until every child had given or collected sticks. Sir Ian gave a gift to any child who still had a stick at the end of the game. How many gifts did he give out?

ANSWER

Sir Ian gave out 10 gifts.

With experience, the student will recognize the need to *look for a pattern*. With one hundred kids in line, it is best to simplify the problem by looking only at the first ten children. By following the data, the solution begins to unfold:

Child 1 hands out sticks to everyone. Children 1, 2, 3, 4, 5, 6, 7, 8, 9, and 10 have sticks.

Child 2 takes sticks away from the even numbers. Now children 1, 3, 5, 7, and 9 have sticks.

Child 3 looks at multiples of 3. He takes the sticks from children 3 and 9 but gives one to child 6. Now children 1, 5, 6, and 7 have sticks.

Child 4 gives one to himself and child 8. Children 1, 4, 5, 6, 7, and 8 have sticks.

Child 5 takes sticks away from himself and child 10. Now children 1, 4, 6, 7, 8, and 10 have sticks.

Child 6 will take his stick away. Children 7 and 8 will do the same on their turns.

Child 9 will give himself a stick on his turn, and child 10 will take his own away when he is supposed to look at multiples of 10.

At this point, after 10 students have performed their duty, children 1, 4, and 9 will have sticks. Problem solvers will recognize this as a *pattern of square numbers.*

Once the pattern is discovered, it becomes clear that 10 children will have sticks at the end of the game: students 1, 4, 9, 16, 25, 36, 49, 64, 81, and 100.

5. QUESTION

At the gym, 371 people use the weight room, 514 use the swimming pool, and 489 play tennis. Of these, 179 people swim and lift weights, 177 play tennis and lift weights, and 184 swim and play tennis. One hundred people do all three. Eighty-nine people do not do any of these activities. How many people go to this gym?

ANSWER

There are 1,023 people who go to the gym.

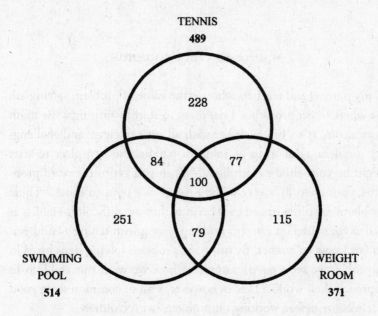

This is a *draw a picture* problem. It requires the use of a Venn diagram. Kids love to use these. The intersecting circles are drawn and labeled. The different sections are used to chart the data. Be careful! When a problem states that "179 people swim and lift weights," it does not mean to place 179 in the section where weights and swimming intersect. Since you have already placed the number 100 in the section where people do all three activities, 100 of the 179 people have already been counted. See the above chart for this example.

Solving daily problems such as these reinforces the culture of our classroom. The work is challenging but fun. The kids feel comfortable making mistakes, knowing help is on the way when the work is difficult. And they get better. They become better thinkers and are motivated not by a test or a grade. They acquire a set of problem-solving skills that will help them for years to come. It's a wonderful way to spend an hour.

Where to Get Problems

Many parents and teachers who see the value of problem solving ask me where to get problems. I tell them to start by visiting www.math stories.com. It's a fun Web site with all sorts of clever and challenging problems. But truth be told, for parents the best place to start might be your child's math book. When you get to the word problems, your child may very well tell you, "We skipped those." These problems are often passed over because they are difficult for adults as well as for students. There is nothing wrong with telling a child you do not know an answer. By using the problem-solving steps listed in the Bible, we set a good example of how we want our children to approach their work. There is, however, a bit of common sense good teachers use before working on problems with children.

Difficult word problems require that teachers do their homework. Good teachers will solve all the problems the night before they teach them. They will scour them for mistakes or ambiguities. But many teachers are not willing to put in the time or effort it takes to teach the problems that will probably be the best challenges for a child.

Every good school-supply store carries problem-solving workbooks for a range of grade levels and abilities. No matter where the problems come from, the process remains the same: Understand the problem, choose an appropriate strategy, solve, and analyze. These fundamental steps will help children solve problems throughout their lives.

Barbara, my brilliant wife, has a question she poses to all my students. We even call it "the Barbara question." It's simple but profound: What will you do when things go wrong? Notice the question does not say *if* things go wrong. Things *will* go wrong. That's a part of life. A person's ability to answer that simple question can mean the difference between success and failure, fulfillment and discontent. The problem-solving steps learned over and over in Room 56 provide the answer to Barbara's question.

Slings and Arrows

My classroom features an elaborate system of professional stage lighting. It was installed by a technician who designs lighting for some of the biggest rock bands in the world. We use the lights to turn Room 56 into a theater for our Shakespeare productions.

One night a local gang broke into our school, a relatively common occurrence. The vandals tore Room 56 apart. They defaced the children's art projects, spray-painted profanity on the walls, and ripped apart our stage lighting. They smashed our two light towers, shattered lightbulbs (expensive ones), and ripped up hundreds of feet of cable.

This took place when my students were on vacation and I was on the East Coast taking former students around to visit colleges. We were touring Brown University in Providence, Rhode Island, when one of the kids back in Los Angeles called me crying. She'd been at the school for orchestra practice and had seen police cars and investigators gathering information about the many classrooms that had been desecrated, including ours. I tried to calm her down by telling her it was only a classroom—that no gang could ever rob her and her classmates of the spirit and work ethic that made them special. I told her not to worry. I was due back next week and would take care of things.

I hung up the phone and tried to put on a brave face for my college-bound students, but inside I was steaming. It was the kind of shock that makes a person think about throwing in the towel. As I drove the students across New York toward Cornell, I thought of the mess that was waiting for me back in L.A.—the hours of cleaning, salvaging, and trying to put the classroom back together.

A week later, still on break, I arrived at school early one morning to begin the process. I entered Room 56 and couldn't believe what I saw. The room was immaculate—in even better shape than I had left it. Kelly, the ten-year-old girl who called me in Rhode Island, had done the stuff that dreams are made on. She told me later she simply collected the data to understand the problem. She called classmates and divided up the work. Some of the kids went to a hardware store and bought special cleansers to get rid of the graffiti. Lucia, another problem solver, put together a team of kids who reorganized the students' papers and folders that had been thrown out of their overturned desks.

This alone would have been amazing. But Sarah, an eleven-year-old former student, was also called in to help. She and her friends rebuilt the light towers. They untangled the cables and rerouted them back to the dimmer board. And for the icing on the cake, she took a bus to find the special bulbs used in stage lighting. After replacing them, she reprogrammed the board using instructions she found online. On the day I returned, she told me she hoped I wouldn't mind, but she had changed some of our lighting sequences. She had made some improvements.

I didn't mind. And even when I am too tired to think, this is what fuels my stamina to arrive early every day. Of course things go wrong in life. They always do. But Room 56 is full of problem solvers. It takes a little extra time to plan this hour before class with my students, but teaching kids to think and solve problems is one of the best gifts we can give them. Whatever life they choose, they will be equipped to negotiate the slings and arrows of outrageous fortune.

THIRTEEN

Celluloid Heroes

It's funny how desperate times can lead to something wonderful. I used to become depressed on Monday mornings when my students would tell me how they had spent their weekends. Many would tell me they had seen a movie. When I asked what they had seen, the answer was usually something like *Johnny Kills Everyone* or *The Slasher Strikes Again*. You get the idea.

I would lecture the children about why these films were inappropriate. They celebrate our baser instincts. Their creators are hurting our society and should not be supported. The films are bad for you. In fact, they are simply bad.

Of course, no one was listening. I can't say that a single kid ever replied to one of my rants with, "Golly, Rafe, thank you for pointing out the error of my ways. I am eternally grateful to you. In the future, I will consult film experts and discuss these matters with my parents before viewing a movie. In this way I will be exposed to true cinematic excellence and improve myself as both a student and a person." Well, you can't blame a person for dreaming.

When I first began teaching, VCRs had just become available. I was the first teacher in school to bring one to class. I still remember the looks I got as I carried it into school. Older teachers didn't know what it was and eyed me with appropriate suspicion. In fact, my motives were harmless: I wanted to show the kids a *Hallmark Hall of Fame* production of *The Count of Monte Cristo*. They had read the novel in class, and I wanted to supplement the experience by showing them the film, which starred Richard Chamberlain, Donald Pleasance, Louis Jourdan, and Tony Curtis as Fernand Mondego (a Frenchman with a Brooklyn accent). The kids stayed after school, and we had a marvelous afternoon watching the movie.

Yet as the kids and I watched more films together, I started to notice a disturbing pattern. Their ability to concentrate for more than a few minutes was quite poor. Their listening skills were weak. When I talked about watching a movie, the kids asked the wrong questions: "Is it black-and-white or color?" "Is it long or short?" "Is it new or old?" I found this disheartening. I wanted them to be asking, "Is it good or bad?"

I realized that if I wanted my students to become true film connoisseurs, I would have to teach the subject with the same vigor and determination with which I taught algebra or Shakespeare. It reminded me that excellence had to be pursued every moment of the day. Watching great films was another opportunity to build on the foundation of merit that I had been constructing in the classroom.

I also became painfully aware that, as with any tool, film can be used for both appropriate and ridiculous means. Since the video (and now DVD) revolution, some teachers regularly show films during class time because they are too lazy to teach. I am astonished by the number of teachers who have deluded themselves into believing that showing films in class is an acceptable replacement for real teaching.

The following example demonstrates this disturbing trend. Toward the end of the school year, the students go through two weeks of standardized testing in reading, writing, math, science, and social studies. Although I have all sorts of reservations about this testing, it is a time we take fairly seriously and students are encouraged to do their best. A DO NOT ENTER sign is placed outside the door of our classroom to make sure the children's concentration will not be disturbed. Yet a few years ago some fifth-graders from another class ignored the sign and burst into my room breathing quite heavily. They were obviously on the run. They were panting and seemed genuinely frightened. It turned out they were running from their classroom. This was the day that their teacher had let the students pick the film they wanted to see. Kids brought in their favorites and the class voted. One of the boys brought in the film that proved to be the winning selection: *Freddy vs. Jason.*

That's right. *Freddy vs. Jason.* This is so wrong, on so many different levels, that it seems absurd to even take it seriously. Why were the parents letting their ten-year-olds watch this? Who bought the film or how did he get it? And the real question: How in the world does an elementary-school teacher convince herself that it's okay to show such a film to her fifth-grade class?

This is an extreme example. To say the least, it doesn't have to be this way. I show my kids terrific films that help them grow in all sorts of meaningful ways. Great movies can help children build character, learn about the impact of good and bad decisions, and be inspired to stand up for their beliefs in difficult situations.

The Weekend Film Club

Many years ago, when I started to give the use of film as a learning tool serious thought, I developed a class option that has become outrageously popular among my students. We call it the Hobart Shakespearean Film Club. The program was carefully designed to improve my students' appreciation and knowledge of film while also sharpening their writing, critical thinking, time management, and responsibility skills. Here's how the club works.

On Fridays, each member of the film club is allowed to borrow a

DVD for the weekend from our in-class library, which has grown over the years into a massive collection (thanks in large part to financial donations from parents who understand that I don't need any more ties, belts, or wallets for Christmas). Club members choose a film and present their Hobart Shakespearean film cards to one of Room 56's DVD monitors. The DVD monitor records the transaction and hands over the film and a sheet of twelve to fifteen questions that I have written about it. Each question must be answered in grammatically correct complete sentences. The sheets of questions are stored in plastic sleeves and must be returned in pristine condition. Students are warned that if they return the questions in shabby condition, they will be suspended from the film club. The same strict rules apply to the DVDs themselves, which must be returned on Monday mornings. Occasionally kids forget them at home. They are suspended from the club for a couple of weeks. Kids learn quickly that taking home films is a privilege and not a right. They earn that privilege by being organized and dependable. Club members learn all sorts of things that have nothing to do with watching movies.

Here is a typical set of questions a club member would take home to answer. These questions correspond to *Charade,* the charming movie called by many "the best Hitchcock film Hitchcock never made."

CHARADE
(1963)

1. In what city does this story take place?
2. What happens to Reggie's husband, Charles?
3. Why were Tex, Gideon, and Scobie chasing Charles Lampert?
4. Why does Peter Joshua confess to Reggie that his real name is Alexander Dyle?

5. What word does Mr. Bartholomew tell Reggie to use instead of "spies"?
6. Why is it funny when Alexander tells Reggie he "met a man with sharp nails"?
7. When the men kidnap Jean Louis, what "treasure" does the little boy find?
8. What happens to Scobie?
9. What happens to Gideon?
10. What was the last thing Tex did before he died?
11. How was Charles hiding the $250,000 he stole from the U.S. government?
12. Who does Mr. Bartholomew turn out to be?
13. How does Peter/Alexander/Adam kill Carson Dyle?
14. What shock does Reggie discover about Adam Canfield?
15. Why does Reggie hope she and Brian have a lot of boys?

Good ideas have a way of naturally evolving into better ones. After a while, my students started to ask if more than one student could work on a film together. Suddenly, the kids were spending time together watching first-rate films, discussing the questions, and practicing their writing. New friendships were formed, and I was astonished to see how quickly the kids began to trust my suggestions. As the students embraced classic films, they began to reject the lackluster new movies our culture tries to push on them. They grew to appreciate the work of Billy Wilder, Sidney Poitier, and Bette Davis. These same students were faster than others to try more difficult literature, art projects, and physical challenges. The film club helped develop an attitude that is attractive in anyone: a curiosity to know more and an appetite for something new.

Tuesdays After School

Every seven days, like hundreds of thousands of unfortunate teachers around the world, I am imprisoned at my school's weekly staff meeting. Ours are held on Tuesday afternoons. Each week we are told about an exciting new technique for teaching language or math—which invariably contradicts the twelve most recent "new techniques" we've been forced to swallow over the past few months. The only thought-provoking element of staff meetings is guessing if the Powers That Be can possibly top the idiocy of the previous week's session. Inevitably, they do.

On these days students are dismissed from school early. Of course they are: Let's take kids who can't read at grade level and whose behavior makes Jack and the tribe in *Lord of the Flies* look like choir boys and *shorten* their school day. That's a brilliant idea!

I found a way to use these shortened days to the children's advantage. Instead of sending the students home at two, I show a great film. The kids can watch the movie and be done by four or four-thirty, when it's still light out. These Tuesday films are an optional activity, of course, but they serve a number of purposes. They are opportunities for students to expand their cinematic knowledge and to exercise their analytical skills. They also tell me which students are willing to choose the more difficult road and sacrifice time after school. I can't be in the room during these films, but many of my former students (who also got out of school early) stop by to watch the movie with the current class. Every kid in the room understands that if he fails to pay attention or acts inappropriately, he will suffer the reasonable punishment of being dismissed from the activity. In fifteen years of Tuesday films, that's never happened. The kids love watching great films in a quiet setting. They watch with a purpose, and the listening skills they cultivate serve them well in countless situations for years to come.

What Films and Where to Get Them

Friday afternoons are always exciting in Room 56. Each student has a list of all the films in our DVD library, and many of the kids will have spent days trying to decide what movie to borrow for the weekend. Of course they don't always end up liking the movies they choose—there is no accounting for taste, after all—but at least they have plenty of options.

Our DVD library currently contains about three hundred films. I started to build it by looking at lists such as the American Film Institute's 100 Greatest American Movies of All Time. Of course, lists like this are only a beginning, and I've never found one I agree with completely. In general, I try to expose the kids to a diverse range of movies in all sorts of genres. My students watch dramas, comedies, westerns, thrillers, fantasies, and foreign films. This past year, fewer than five of my incoming students had seen *The Wizard of Oz,* fewer than ten had seen *E.T.,* and, to my complete shock, practically none of them knew that the *Star Wars* series began in 1977. By the end of the year, these same students knew why Steven Spielberg so admires Akira Kurosawa.

But beware. As I mentioned before, there is no accounting for taste. I found that out the hard way one year when I let a top student named Pablo borrow Peter Weir's film *Witness.* I figured a Harrison Ford action thriller would be a good way to introduce a bright twelve-year-old to the mysteries of Amish life. Man, was that a mistake!

The next Monday, Pablo's mother was in my classroom, furious that I would allow her son to see such "trash." She was shocked that I would expose him to "the bad scene." At first I didn't know what she was talking about, but then I remembered a scene in which Harrison Ford's character, a Philadelphia cop named John Book—who shares a mutual attraction with the lovely Kelly McGillis, who plays an Amish woman named Rachel—accidentally sees Rachel washing herself and gets a very good look at her breasts. The two stare at each other, and Book withdraws, knowing a relationship between the two would be impossible.

As Pablo's mother stood before me demanding answers, I regretted that I had not considered her point of view. At the same time, I recalled an earlier scene in the movie in which two evil police officers slit a man's throat in a train station bathroom (it's interesting to see the great Danny Glover play a villain in his earlier days!). I found it curious that Pablo's mom would find a beautiful woman's breasts more objectionable than a gruesome murder, but I knew better than to argue with her. In any case, she gave me an earful and scurried from the room because—and I swear I'm not making this up—her priest was scheduled to give her younger daughter an exorcism later that morning. This fact drove home the lesson that not all families see things from my point of view. Incidentally, upon hearing that the woman's daughter was being exorcised, it took all of my willpower to refrain from calling after her, "Exorcised? Have I got a film for *you*!"

In all seriousness, however, this incident taught me to be mindful that different families have different moral compasses. I immediately instituted a system by which the parents of each student tell me exactly what kinds of films their children are allowed to watch. Some students in film club watch nothing but G-rated films. Others are allowed to see movies that are rated PG-13. Some of my former students are permitted to watch R-rated films because their parents deem it okay. The important thing here is to keep your eye on the ball. It's natural that different families have different boundaries. Your job is to get excellent films in front of the students—and to inspire them to watch, listen, and write about them.

Traditions

Here are a few films my students watch with me each year. Naturally, these movies will not be appropriate for kids of all ages. They are simply films that I have used with success in my fifth-grade classroom.

Twelve Angry Men   This is the first film we watch as a class. It's a brilliant drama with no special effects that always changes my students' view of what makes a film great.

High Noon   As with all great westerns, there is more here than the West. This film reinforces the importance of a personal moral code—even in situations when no one else seems to have one.

The Crossing   This is not a great film, but it's a wonderful supplement to any unit on the Revolutionary War.

The Wizard of Oz   There's no place like home.

A Hard Day's Night   It's still about the best movie about the joy of music ever filmed.

Field of Dreams   This is one of the great baseball movies. We watch this about a week before the World Series begins.

Wait Until Dark	We watch this thriller near Halloween. The kids see why Audrey Hepburn was a star, cringe at Alan Arkin's creepy villain, and get scared to death by one of the great cheap-shot moments in film!
Saving Private Ryan	We watch this a week before Veterans Day. The kids never forget Tom Hanks's directive "Earn this." My students repeat this line throughout the school year.
Planes, Trains and Automobiles	We watch this movie on the Wednesday afternoon before Thanksgiving. We have dinner afterward. For many of my students, it is their first Thanksgiving meal.
The Civil War	This Ken Burns/PBS film is a fabulous supplement to our study of the Civil War. We also watch *Glory* and the Turner production of *Gettysburg* (based on Michael Shaara's novel *The Killer Angels*).
It's a Wonderful Life	Every December 23, we watch George Bailey learn life's greatest lesson.
Groundhog Day	In February, the kids die laughing and actually learn about the holiday in one afternoon.

Casablanca	We watch this every Valentine's Day. *Here's looking at you, kids!*
Of Mice and Men	We watch the Gary Sinise–John Malkovich version after finishing Steinbeck's novel.
Malcolm X	This is the perfect way to celebrate finishing the audio book. It is fantastic to hear Ossie Davis recite the brilliant eulogy he spoke so many years ago.
Mr. Smith Goes to Washington	This film is a terrific supplement to our unit on the Constitution and U.S. government.
To Kill a Mockingbird	This is the last book we read every year and the last film we watch. Every year the kids cry during the book, cry during the film, and I make a fool of myself and cry too.

These are just suggestions. As a parent or teacher, you can create your own lists and your own madness. But watch *with* the kids. Inspire them. Set an example by watching films quietly and thoughtfully. You never know where your efforts will lead.

For instance, when I started the film club I couldn't have imagined how much impact it would have on a kid like Frank, who was a student in Room 56 many years ago. Frank was a good but not outstanding student. He did his work, followed the path of least resistance, and stayed out of trouble. Nothing in his work or manner suggested his life could be extraordinary—until the film club touched a nerve.

He simply loved it. Actually, *loved* is not a strong enough word. This kid devoured films at the rate of three or four a weekend. He not only answered questions but wrote volumes about everything. I had never seen such passion. His pencil had a sort of electric energy that brought to mind van Gogh's *Starry Night*.

Over the course of our year together, we had two astonishing conversations on different Mondays. The first one was short.

Frank: (Handing in questions on Akira Kurosawa's *Rashomon*) *Rafe, do you think* Rashomon *was Kurosawa's best film? I think* Yojimbo *was better.*

Rafe: (Flustered) *Well, gee, Frank, I don't know. They're both good.*

Frank: (Walking away) *Well,* Yojimbo *was better . . .*

He was ten years old.

A few weeks later, I asked him how he spent the weekend. For the first time in months, he had not taken home a movie.

Rafe: *Hey, Frank, how was your weekend?*

Frank: *Great! My mom took me to the Czechoslovakian film festival in Venice Beach.*

Rafe: *You went to the Czechoslovakian film festival?*

Frank: (Impatient) *Have you ever seen a Czechoslovakian film?*

Rafe: (Mumbling) *Well, actually . . . uh . . .*

Frank: *They make some very fine films.*

Rafe: (The idiot teacher) *Jeez, Frank, you love films so much you should be a film critic one day.*

Frank: (The wise student) *Critic? Critics don't do anything. When
        I grow up I'm going to be a* filmmaker.

Today Frank attends NYU film school. I never did much of anything for this boy. We got along fine—we both loved baseball—but
I did not make him smarter, nicer, or better in any way. I just threw
a few films in his direction, and apparently that made all the difference. He knows it, too. Every Christmas, Frank sends a film to be
added to our collection.

FOURTEEN

Goin' Mobile

One night my students and I were walking down D Street in Washington, D.C., to have dinner at the Hard Rock Cafe. The kids love it. The atmosphere is fun and the waiters are nice. And as musicians, the kids enjoy looking at all the memorabilia. There were about thirty students with me. When we walked in, a friendly host came over.

Host: *Wow, you've gotta have the toughest job in the world. All these kids!*

Rafe: *It's not that hard. Don't worry, they're well behaved.*

Host: *The bar is over there. We'll handle it.*

Rafe: *Excuse me?*

Host: *You know, the bar . . .*

Rafe: *Actually, I don't know . . .*

Host: *Well, we get a lot of schools here. The teachers go into the bar for a drink while the kids run around the restaurant.*

Rafe: *Thanks, but we do things a little differently.*

Indeed we do. There is nothing I like better than taking the kids on the road, whether it is an afternoon trip to a museum or a two-week tour through Washington, D.C., and Virginia. Too often, teachers view road trips as vacations; I see them as invaluable opportunities to augment the teaching I do in the classroom. Trips with Room 56 are unique. The activities are meticulously planned, the kids are extraordinarily well prepared, and the objectives are always clear. I want our trips to teach the students lessons they will use for the rest of their lives.

Why the Road?

That's a very good question. Anyone who has ever traveled to a place like Washington, D.C., has had the unpleasant experience of seeing children out of control. Last year, I was in the Smithsonian's National Air and Space Museum and entered a bathroom that a middle school group was just exiting. The children were laughing because they had actually smeared feces all over the toilet seats. No teachers were in sight. When I complained to the museum guards and asked them to do something about the group, a nice man shrugged his shoulders and told me, "All my time is spent in security at the door to stop terrorists. Once the kids are inside there isn't much I can do about it."

This is what class trips have become. Our social and educational systems are deteriorating. The kids who came out of that bathroom will return home and tell friends and relatives they visited Washington, D.C. Many will respond, "How nice." What those friends and relatives may not realize is that today's museums and historic places are filled with young people who wander aimlessly or are led by equally clueless adults.

It doesn't have to be this way. My class trips are designed to accomplish two clear and important objectives: First, Hobart Shakespeareans are expected to pursue knowledge with a passion and depth of understanding that separates them from mediocre students. As they enter the Lincoln Memorial, they know a great deal about the man, his temple, and the reason he is remembered. If they are attending a production of *The Tempest* at the Folger Shakespeare Library, they have read the play in such depth that they are ready to praise or criticize the production with knowledgeable opinions based on thorough study. I do not want my students to be mediocre.

Second, I use trips to prepare them for the college environment. I believe that many of today's elementary, middle, and high schools are making a small but significant mistake in how they think about college. They place so much emphasis on *getting in* to college that they lose sight of the larger issue of *finishing* college. As a result, a shocking percentage of college students never attain degrees. Why does this happen? It can't be because they weren't smart enough. These are the kids who by definition have been successful in school. These are the kids with the good grades, the high test scores, and the right extracurricular activities. Did they suddenly become too stupid to pass their classes? Of course not. After all, passing English Lit is a piece of cake for these kids. Yet learning what to do when it's Saturday night and two papers are due on Monday *and* you have a fever *and* your mother isn't there with the Tylenol is often a different story. Truth is, many kids simply haven't learned enough about life to survive the college experience. Handling money, relationships, loneliness, difficult people, and disappointment can all be factors that defeat kids who are on their own for the first time. I use road trips to teach the students in Room 56 the skills they will need when they are on their own one day. The Hobart Shakespeareans make it to college and finish. It all begins with trips outside the classroom.

The Readiness Is All

A few years ago a friend of mine who teaches at a school outside California led a high school field trip to the West Coast. I was very surprised to hear him complain about their day at Disneyland. He told me the kids were all bored. Now, anyone who has ever been to the Magic Kingdom on a hot and crowded day has discovered that Disneyland is not always "the happiest place on earth," but I had never heard it described as *boring*. I was curious about what had gone wrong. I asked my friend all about their trip and, perhaps more important, their preparations for the trip. Take a look at some of the differences between his class and Room 56:

- The high school kids had learned nothing about the history of Disneyland.
- ★ The kids in Room 56 had read *Birnbaum's Disneyland* guidebook and received maps of the Magic Kingdom.

- The high school group did not like the Jungle Cruise ride.
- ★ The kids in Room 56 loved it. They prepared for it by watching *The African Queen*. When the ride was over they discussed similarities and differences between the movie and the ride.

- The high school group enjoyed the drops on Splash Mountain.
- ★ The kids in Room 56 loved the drops and sang along with the music. They recognized the characters from watching

Song of the South and had even written essays on the racism in that movie.

- The high school group thought Mr. Toad's Wild Ride was stupid.
- ★ The kids in Room 56 had read *The Wind in the Willows* and looked for their favorite characters.

- The high school group did not attend the exhibit Great Moments with Mr. Lincoln.
- ★ The kids in Room 56 had watched Ken Burns's *Civil War* and loved the exhibit. Their favorite part was a letter from Lincoln to General McClellan that they had read and studied in school.

- The high school group's meals were paid for by the dozen chaperones who accompanied them on the trip.
- ★ The kids in Room 56 learned to be careful with their money by paying for their own meals. None of the children ran out—they had planned their food budgets in advance.

You get the idea.

When I think about the enormous expense of taking my students on a trip, my first instinct is to hop over to my local bookstore and spend $15 to $20 on a good travel guide. I learn everything I can about our destination. I find out when it will be least crowded. I check weather patterns and special exhibits that may be of interest. The kids also look through these books. They absorb as much information as I can get in front of their eyes.

By the time the trip rolls around, I have little work to do. More important, the kids are primed to get the most out of it. They have trained to be ready. They know what rides or exhibits to seek out.

They've planned their meals. They've gotten plenty of sleep the night before. They've applied their Six Levels to their travels. If an elderly person wants to get an ice cream, the kids "part the waters" and allow the person to get in front of them. It's not a rule. It's who they are. These trips provide an opportunity for young people to engage with the wider world and to discover the best in themselves.

My coworker Andrew Hahn, one of the great art teachers in the nation, has accompanied my students on trips and applied our philosophy to his own outstanding program. Nothing gets Andy more excited than taking his kids to the Los Angeles County Museum of Art. Like all good teachers, Andy helps his kids become extraordinary. We've all seen youngsters running wild around a museum; Andy sees a trip to the museum as an entirely different sort of adventure.

Because he works with poor children, many of whose families do not own cars, Andy decided to supplement his museum trips with lessons on the wonders of public transportation. Andy tested the bus and rail system (not easy in Los Angeles!) and figured out the best route to the museum. He uses public transportation even though he could easily find people to drive his kids. Suddenly it's more than a field trip—Andy's kids learn to navigate the world outside their windows. They no longer feel trapped in their apartments. They start spending Saturdays in libraries or museums. They know how to get there. Their teacher has shown them the way.

When Andy's kids get to the museum, they always have a purpose. They understand the museum's layout—each student is given a map—and they know which artworks they want to see. Sometimes they look at only one or two paintings. They usually take out their sketchbooks and try to draw the paintings for themselves. They understand the artists they are emulating. The students groan when it is time to go home.

Finding the Money

It costs money to take kids out. Sometimes it costs a lot of money. There is a reason this chapter is in the "Madness" section of this book. Spending lots of money on students is for the most committed teachers—and those who should be!

In my early years, I supplied all the money. That was a mistake. I worked afternoon jobs, night jobs, weekend jobs—anything to make a dollar for the class. I tended bathrooms during rock concerts. I worked for an ice cream company arranging their merchandise in market displays, delivered newspapers for the *Los Angeles Times*, drove for messenger services, and tutored rich kids in Beverly Hills. I hated all of it. But I was determined to show my students the life they were working for.

I learned three things from working extra jobs. First, I learned that all of my students should pay *something* when I take them on a trip. If you give people something for nothing, they usually get nothing out of it. Whether they pay $1 or $100, even my poorest students make some contribution to the trip. Second, I learned that working multiple jobs destroys even the healthiest of people. I wore myself ragged. I had the money to take kids places, but I was too ill or fatigued to do a good job leading the trips.

Finally, I learned that we are not in this alone. Money is available from a variety of foundations, community organizations, and individuals. Be advised that, at least in the beginning, patrons may be reluctant to finance trips, which are often perceived to have short-term results. You will have better luck raising money for more permanent items such as computers, musical instruments, and science equipment. In any event, patrons will not give money to a classroom unless it is registered with the government as an official 501(c)(3) nonprofit organization.

Registering as a nonprofit will cost money. Lawyers can set it up for you. In my case, the cause was spearheaded by an angel on my shoulder, my former student Matt Parlow. A graduate of Yale and now a law professor himself, Matt was and remains the guiding force behind the Hobart Shakespearean Fund. If you don't have a friend like Matt, it's worth contacting a few law firms to see if you can find a nice attorney who will do this for you and take only one leg or arm.

Once you have your nonprofit status, concentrate on your classroom itself. Do not think about extended travel for the first few years. Establish a fabulous place of learning. When potential patrons see your class in action, they might very well want to help you out. Use your early grants for extra books, computers, and science materials. Baseball gloves are a better investment than baseball games. As a dedicated teacher, you have years to establish a terrific travel program. My class did not do a lot of travel in the beginning; I was focused on creating a magical classroom from the ground up.

Washington, D.C.:
U.S. History and So Much More

Families and school groups love to visit our nation's capital. My class does it every year. Here are a few helpful tips for planning a trip to Washington. They are the product of many years of trial and error.

When to Go

It might not be possible, but try to go during unusual times of the year. In the summer, it is miserably hot and humid. The weather can have a serious effect on the mood of the kids. Also, if at all possible, do not go during spring break. I know the cherry blossoms are beautiful and all that, but the city will be packed with student groups. Most of them behave terribly. Museums and monuments are overrun with out-of-control kids and exhausted group leaders.

My class goes to Washington in late October or early November. It's a beautiful time of year, and our year-round school is on break during these weeks. The city is quiet, and other school groups are few and far between. It is a much better environment for instilling civility in your kids. Our trip is exciting, of course, but we never treat it as an earth-shattering, once-in-a-lifetime event. I want my students to think of travel as something they will do often in their lives.

Preparation

Who goes on such trips? With all due respect to the popular "No Child Left Behind" cry, I leave kids behind all the time. My school year begins in July, and students who want to make the trip to Washington are required to spend time preparing for it on Friday and Saturday afternoons throughout the summer and fall. Some kids do not want to put in the extra hours. That's fine with me. It is my job to open the door; students are welcome to walk through it or not. But the trip is only for students who are willing to put in the work to *earn* their place on the plane.

Our preparation sessions are always divided into two periods: first, history lessons about the places we will visit, and second, lessons about life away from home. On a typical Friday after school, we spend the first hour on history we have not covered in class. We watch documentaries about the presidential memorials and Arlington National Cemetery and study the destinations we will visit in great detail. For instance, when we talk about the Lincoln Memorial, I download the inscription of Lincoln's Second Inaugural Address that is etched into the monument's wall. The students read it and watch the PBS series *The Civil War*. We study the Kennedy years and learn about that awful day in Dallas and the grim weeks that followed. When the students approach JFK's grave in Arlington, they will be somber. They know about him. They recognize the excerpts from his inaugural address that are etched near his grave—we have studied the speech on Friday afternoons. They quickly identify his brother's grave nearby and reread the speech he made in Indianapolis the night Martin Luther King Jr. was murdered. When they walk up the hill to Arlington House, the longtime home of Robert E. Lee, they enter it with respect—not for fear of breaking some rule, but because they genuinely respect the building.

The second hour of our sessions is spent preparing for life on the road. The kids know who their roommates will be. They have decided who will shower in the morning or who will shower at night. They've seen diagrams of their hotel rooms and know where they will put their things. Five or six students stay in a suite, which has two queen beds and a sofa bed in the living room.

I have discovered that teaching young people to behave appropriately in a hotel is one of the more difficult tasks facing a parent or teacher. Restaurants are easy because the kids are surrounded by people behaving properly. It is tougher when they are in a hotel room and do not realize that noise might disturb other people.

I encourage the kids to use the Six Levels as a guide to hotel etiquette. As a result, Hobart Shakespeareans do not talk in hallways. We rarely watch television in hotel rooms. We can do that back home in Los Angeles. Rooms are used to read, play games (Scrabble is a favorite), and write letters. When using the bathroom, students close but do not lock doors. Locked doors might be accidentally closed upon leaving the bathroom and result in locking out room-mates. The kids trust each other and know that a closed door is not to be touched. When a bathroom is free, the door is left open. Students are taught to leave a thank-you note and tip for their maids before going out for the day. Since, as fire prevention, hotel doors are designed to slam shut, my students learn to close their room doors carefully and quietly when they leave their rooms so as not to disturb other guests.

Here are a few more things the kids in Room 56 learn before they go on an extended trip.

Airplanes

1. The children know how to line up alphabetically by last name at the ticket counter to check luggage.
2. They understand how to store their belongings on the plane, both in the overhead compartment and on the floor under the seat in front of them.
3. They know how long the flight will take and plan how to spend the time. Most of it is spent reading and doing crossword puzzles or puzzles about the places they will be seeing.
4. They know how to politely order food and drinks from flight attendants.
5. They know where the bathrooms are and how to use them. This includes how to lock the door properly and where to stand if the bathroom is occupied.
6. They know how to deplane. The rows in front of them always go first.

Hotel Rooms

1. The students know how to use electronic keys.
2. They know their first job is to check the back of their door to find out where the fire exit is located.
3. They have their room assignments before the trip. Two students in each room have been chosen to keep room keys with them at all times.
4. Dirty towels are placed neatly on the bathroom floor.
5. Dirty laundry is placed in plastic bags or pillowcases that students bring and keep in their closet. On extended trips, students do their own laundry. In order to avoid long waits for washers and dryers, only one room does its laundry each night.
6. Students modulate their voices at all times.
7. Students know how to use their heater or air-conditioning unit properly.
8. Students know how to locate ice machines.
9. Occasionally we order room service. With five or six students to a room, the kids learn to write down the entire order before picking up the phone. One student speaks clearly and requests the food.
10. At night, we all get together to talk about the next day. When students return to their rooms, they call to let me know they have arrived safely. They know how to lock their door.

Recently, some former students and I shared a laugh. They had just come back from a middle school trip to Washington, D.C., with their new school. They stayed in a hotel and were informed that tape would be placed across their doors at night so their teachers would know if they sneaked out. This has never happened on a Hobart Shakespearean trip. I trust my students and they trust me. They do not leave their hotel rooms at night because they understand it might be dangerous. If you don't trust your kids to behave, they shouldn't be traveling with you. They simply aren't ready.

Where We Stay

When traveling with a large group of students, we usually stay at an Embassy Suites. The rooms are large and clean, and the extra living room area allows us to put five or six students in a room. The chain's main attraction, however, is its breakfast.

Breakfast is the most difficult meal to serve to a large group of students. Embassy Suites offers an enormous complimentary buffet breakfast with every kind of food imaginable: eggs, omelets, potatoes, breads, pancakes, French toast, waffles, cereals, fruits, juices, and more—perfect for a large group. As I am teaching the kids to be independent, the children do not have to eat together. Individual students come down to breakfast whenever they like. They've been trained to get their food and sit down at a table to eat. The kids have been told the night before what time we are leaving the hotel for our day's activities. We usually leave between eight and nine in the morning. Students plan their mornings accordingly. They have to estimate the time they will need to wash, dress, eat, tidy up their rooms, and prepare for the day. In twenty years of trips, I have never had a student oversleep or be late for the day.

Crossing the Street

There is one phone call I plan to never make. Tragically, every year, students are killed on class trips. I know people who have had to make that call home to a parent. I will never make this call. I understand that my attention to safety might seem a bit crazy, but I don't care. My students must be safe.

I actually keep a file of newspaper clippings about school accidents and show them to the students. Some of these tragedies are freak accidents, such as lightning strikes or avalanches. In these terrible instances, one can feel heartbreak but not guilt. But my file also contains many articles that are tragic because a child's death could have been prevented. Most of these involve crossing streets.

I often see school groups crossing the street in a line with one adult at the front and one at the back. Several articles in my file tell tragic stories that resulted from this street-crossing procedure. In most cases, students in the middle of the line are struck by a car. When Room 56 crosses a street, we follow two procedures. First, no child may *ever* step off a curb before I give him the green light. Second, I go out into the street and stop traffic completely. Even if I am standing in the middle of Pennsylvania Avenue at rush hour, I go out and stop all traffic. Only when every car in the vicinity is stopped do the kids step into the street.

On a recent trip to Washington, the students were walking back from the Jefferson Memorial toward the Mall. It was midafternoon and about thirty of us were making our way to the Smithsonian Metro station. Many of the kids were walking in front of me when they came to a crosswalk. The light flashed green, yet the kids did not step off the curb. They know better. They were waiting for me to get to the front and stop traffic. As these children waited, a car screamed through the opposing red light and slammed into the rear of a car just across the intersection, not fifteen feet from the kids. The shrieking of the brakes and the deafening bang of the collision jolted the students. They were shaken and immediately looked at me. It's not a game. Had these children stepped off the curb with the light green, they would have been following the law. They also would've been dead. I trust my students. It's everyone else I don't trust.

Photographs

Here's a little tip about taking pictures. When you plan your day, look at a map and chart where the sun will be. Schedule your activities so that when you are outdoors the sun will be behind the person taking the pictures. For example, in Washington, D.C., it's best to take pictures at the Lincoln Memorial earlier in the day. At the other end of the Mall, the Capitol will look its best later in the day. These photographs will be an important part of the students' memories. A little extra planning will help the pictures bring smiles to the faces of the children and their families for years to come.

Less Is More

When planning a student trip, group leaders often place too much emphasis on the itinerary and not enough on the students themselves. Parents and teachers want the children to see as much as possible and wind up running the kids ragged in an attempt to cram in every available sight and learning experience. An experienced group leader knows that if the itinerary is too crowded, the students actually learn less instead of more. Young people get tired, and even the best and most energetic students have saturation points. A good group leader understands that less is more.

When my students and I are in the capital, we do far less than other groups. I usually plan two activities a day. After breakfast, we spend about ninety minutes at a museum or monument. Keep in mind that each sight has been studied in detail in the months preceding the trip, so every activity is relevant and meaningful. Our morning activity is followed up by a good lunch. I want the kids to eat in a pleasant environment with plenty of healthy selections. Favorite spots include the lunch areas in the Smithsonian museums. Both the National Museum of Natural History and the National Museum of American History also run excellent food courts with salads, soups, and fresh fruits and vegetables. The National Gallery of Art is another good place to eat. If you are using the Metro, try stopping off at Union Station. Its enormous food court caters to federal employees, and its selections are far better than typical fast food, cuisines ranging from Greek to Thai to Mexican.

These lunches are expensive. The kids can save money by carrying water bottles. Most students save a piece of fruit from breakfast to eat at lunch. However, even though eating in museums can be costly, the extra expense is worth every penny. The kids get the opportunity to learn about making healthy selections rather than grabbing a hot dog (and an inevitable stomachache) at the corner vendor (a mistake I made when I first took students to Washington). After a quality lunch, the students have enough energy for a successful afternoon activity.

Changing Lives on the Road

Several years ago, the kids and I returned from our annual Washington trip. I had made a conscious effort to remind myself several times a day that less is more. We saw fewer monuments and museums on this trip than in the past. We probably learned less history. But the kids ate better, laughed more often, and slept longer hours.

Upon our return, a group of teachers visited Room 56 and had lunch with the children. There was an adorable little girl in class, fragile and sweet, who was talking with some of them. They asked her, "What was your favorite thing about your trip to Washington?"

They expected her to answer with something like "The Lincoln Memorial" or "The Air and Space Museum." She didn't, but her answer indicated I was getting my priorities straight. Her answer was, "My favorite thing about Washington is that Rafe took good care of me."

I love being a teacher. You have the chance to get better at what you do. From this simple one-line evaluation I have learned to use the road to do some of my best teaching. One year I took former students to New York to tour college campuses. In doing so, I spent most of my energy making sure the high school kids with me felt relaxed. With the enormous pressure of the college admissions process looming, the last thing these students needed was a "Let's see twelve campuses in five days" tour.

I did a lot of listening on this trip. I gave advice only if asked. In my earliest years, I would return from such trips exhausted. Students rarely thanked me, and, truth be told, they probably didn't get as much from our trips as they should have. Now the kids were saying I took good care of them. And after the most recent college trip, one of my students wrote to me. For all the times I have struck out as a teacher, it's nice to hit the occasional home run.

> *Dear Rafe,*
>
> *Words cannot describe the gratitude I am feeling right now. I'd like to thank you for everything—for driving the van for literally five hours every day, making reservations, knowing what you're doing, not getting lost, showing us a variety of select colleges, informing us with brief baseball lectures, taking us to Yankee Stadium, interesting us with your crazy stories and jokes, taking me to Tiffany's, showing us around and visiting the tourist sites, buying us college souvenirs, taking us out to dinner at Tavern on the Green and the Hard Rock Cafe, making sure we were never late, getting the best hotel rooms, keeping us safe, giving us options and the freedom to choose what we want to do, and always being such a wonderful teacher, friend, and role model. I can never stress enough the fact that I would never be the person that I am and experience what I have without you. That is why I am and will always be forever grateful.*

I appreciate you helping me find and look for the college that is right for me. After so many information seminars, I feel like I really know what is expected and required for the admission process. I always realized there are so many factors that also affect and determine my decision in choosing a college, such as location, environment, size, and weather. Through this amazing trip (with just about the most amazing people) I was able to learn so much about myself. I really enjoyed visiting Columbia University because I found their curriculum and campus to perfectly suit what I was looking for in a college. I am so excited about going to college now! The fear went away!

Also, Happy Father's Day! Even if you may not be my "real" dad, I just wanted to let you know that you've always played a father figure in my life, such that you were able to do the things for me that my dad could not. I'm so grateful for so many things you have done for me. You have taught me useful information, shown me the world, allowed me to perform, molded/influenced me into the person I am right now, and shown me much kindness. Thank you for always thinking about me wherever you are, and letting me know with the usual postcards. You have definitely helped me to become and strive to be a better person every day.

Sincerely,

Joanna

Dorothy was right. There is no place like home. But after learning from my mistakes, I see that life on the road can be pretty good, too.

FIFTEEN

It's Only Rock 'n' Roll (but I Like It)

Room 56 rocks. People often write to me and mistakenly compare us to the hilarious Jack Black and the kids in the movie *School of Rock*. It was a cute film, but the kids in Hobart Shakespeareans take *all* of their studies seriously. We are dedicated to excellence in all things. Room 56 rocks, but the students also read, write, and calculate far beyond expectations.

We didn't always rock. In fact, in the beginning, we didn't play music. We occasionally sang a song at a school assembly, but so did other classrooms. Over the years our program evolved, step by step, into its present form. Today my students can play practically anything, from Muddy Waters to Radiohead. More important, they understand the music they play. In Room 56, reading music is taken as seriously as reading itself.

Start Me Up

All my students are given the opportunity to learn how to read music. We do this during our recess and lunch periods in the first few weeks of school. We use guitars, but that's only one way. I have several friends who do the same thing with recorders. They are cheaper and easier to store. We use the guitar only because it's the instrument I happen to know how to play.

I have visited music classes in which students aren't taught to read music. They "learn" to play instruments but never understand what they are doing. In many cases, they can't even tune their instruments. I reject this methodology. Although putting together a rock band is certainly an act of madness, there must be a method in it. I want the kids to be lifelong musicians, not trained seals performing for some school function. In Room 56, the students learn to read music by playing scales. Before long they move on to playing simple classical pieces.

A young teacher once visited me from a school with a renowned music program. He watched us rehearse some songs that the kids would perform later in the year for our Shakespeare production. He loved the songs, but he had a few questions:

Teacher: *So you'll use these songs for* The Merry Wives of Windsor?

Rafe: *Yeah, aren't they great?*

Teacher: *I love it, but I don't understand . . . Are you doing the same play next year?*

Rafe: *Next year I think we'll do* Henry IV.

Teacher: *I don't get it. How can this music match* Henry IV?

Rafe: *Well, it doesn't. We'll pick new songs.*

Teacher: *You can do that?*

Rafe: *Of course you can. Why not?*

Teacher: *At our school we do the same songs every year.*

Of course they do. The kids cannot read music, so they are taught a simple set of songs. As kids move to higher grades, they remain with the "orchestra" but do not have the skills to learn new material. The teacher is busy showing the new students the same songs learned the year before. The returning students cannot go ahead on their own

because they have no knowledge of how to proceed. Imagine if reading were taught this way. In order for a child to move on to other books, he has to understand the fundamentals of reading. The same is true for music.

Any sheet-music store or online site sells all sorts of books of simple classical music. Bach's pieces translate especially well for the guitar. Once the kids can play some basic melodies, divide them into groups and let them try pieces written for duets, trios, and quartets. Young people may not normally listen to classical music, but once they play it, they're hooked. Even my most ardent rockers and rappers love to play classical music. Vivaldi is a class favorite.

Did the Guitars Grow on Trees?

If you want to teach your students to play guitar, you have a number of decisions to make. First of all, if you work with students who are impoverished, where do you get guitars? I began by making friends with small music-store owners in my community. They were willing to sell me cheap used guitars. I often paid between $50 and $100 for one. Students and their families were sometimes willing to buy their own. They would go to these owners, tell them "Rafe sent me," and get taken care of. In the early days, students shared guitars. Today I have more guitars than I need, even though I teach as many as forty classical guitarists at the lesson during recess.

When students buy their own guitars, they often ask me if they should get nylon or steel strings. It really depends on their goals. If classical music is the student's main focus, nylon is definitely the way to go. If the student wants to play pop music, steel is the better choice.

You can always find cheap electric guitars, but that's not my style. We practice on simple guitars, but for performances we bring out the heavy artillery. The Fender Stratocaster is perhaps the most versatile electric guitar. Another favorite in Room 56 is the classic Rickenbacker, whose chimelike sound is great for playing music by artists such as the Beatles, the Byrds, Tom Petty, and John Fogerty. Ovation makes a nice acoustic guitar that plugs in and sounds great with any band. The funniest sight in my class might be watching ten-year-old children play Fender Jazz Bass guitars that are bigger than they are. But when the audience hears the kids play, they stop laughing.

And Your Bird Can Sing

Believe it or not, my singing ability is even worse than my artistic ability. I sometimes joke with the kids that if I were to break into song, their exodus from the classroom would rival that of the Israelites fleeing Egypt. Despite this sad reality, many of my students sing well. How do they do it?

I have learned over the years that many students simply haven't developed their ears. With practice, they can actually get better at hearing notes. I know this is true from personal experience. As a child, I had difficulty tuning a guitar without a piano or tuning aid. These days, I can tune a guitar quite well by ear. It's simply that I've done it hundreds of times and the sound of the notes is ingrained in my musically deficient brain.

When my students want to sing a song, I start by burning the song onto a CD for each child. This allows the kids to sing along at home instead of spending valuable class time. Once the kids know the melody and lyrics, we choose a key. Very few rock songs are sung in keys comfortable for the children. I usually take out a guitar and play the song with simple chords. We begin in the key sung by the band. The kids will start laughing. It's usually too low for them. There's nothing funnier than listening to a ten-year-old girl try to sing in a key meant for a twenty-five-year-old man. By using a capo, I change the key a few times until the kids find a comfortable zone for their voices.

Students love to sing harmonies. It's a gift. Some children struggle at it, but each year I have a few students who are amazing at picking out harmonies. By dividing a song up into a melody line and one or more harmonies, you get to involve more students. The kids feel more necessary. When everyone sings melody, many children are thinking, *I don't really have to sing this. With fifteen other kids singing, who would notice if I wasn't here?* By singing in harmony, the students learn more about music, improve their listening and singing skills, and feel better about their own contributions to a song.

In Room 56 we have a sound board with four microphones. We spend hours trying different combinations of student singers. Any child who wants to sing is given a chance. They learn that four students singing on key may not be enough to make a song special. We experiment with different combinations of singers to find a magic blend of voices. The best rock and pop groups find a way to create unique sounds—from the Beach Boys to the Temptations to Nirvana to Green Day. This process of experimentation can be thrilling for the kids. Every so often we have a "musical eureka" when the singers try something new and everyone screams, "That's it!" Every triumph motivates the kids to dig deeper, stretch further, and attempt even more difficult songs. It's a never-ending process through which students constantly experiment, learn, and have fun.

One last piece of advice about changing the key of music: Although a capo can change the key on a guitar, and the key of an electronic keyboard can be changed with the push of a button, these shortcuts deprive students of the opportunity to play in different keys. Once we have chosen the key in which we will perform a song, we play in that key. It is sometimes harder, but the children become better musicians, and that's the point.

Scoring Music and the Danger of the Internet

I love the Internet. It has changed all of our lives, often for the better. I remember my early days of teaching, in the 1980s. If I wanted to teach the kids a poem by Walt Whitman, I went to the library and made copies. Teaching the periodic table of elements meant a Saturday-morning trip to the teacher supply store to buy a poster for our bulletin board. Those days vanished with the Internet—everything is a keystroke away.

However, that's not always a good thing. In the early days of Room 56's rock band, I mistakenly believed I had found a good tool on the Internet. Hundreds of Web sites offer free musical "tablature"—a simplified system of musical notation that helps beginning guitarists play the lead and bass lines of their favorite rock and pop songs. The problem is that very little Internet tablature is musically correct. It usually *resembles* the song in question, but in an off-key, oversimplified sort of way. Also, there is precious little editing or oversight on the Internet. Any yahoo (pardon the pun) can write down what he wants, rant about his life, or start a Web site called www.lincolnwasanazi.com and get away with it.

You need to consider the source. I found mine in a professional musician who gives guitar lessons at a music store. You can do the same. If you are a lover of music but have no ability, get help. Most music stores employ professional music teachers—that's how I met Dan, an amazing musician who scores our music. With the help of Dan and a computer, my students do not sound *like* Green Day—for all intents and purposes, they *are* Green Day. I do not have Dan's musical talent, but when I consider the hundreds of unpaid hours I spend helping the kids rock, I figure I might as well do it correctly.

All of the students learn the complete score. By using rock lines that are musically correct, the kids learn to play like the pros. In addition, their ability to read and play classical music allows them to learn pop songs incredibly quickly. Show me a kid who can play all three movements of Vivaldi's Concerto in D Major (as my ten-year-olds do), and I'll show you a student who can play U2 well and in a matter of days.

Keyboards and Drums

When I look back at the early days of our rock band, I laugh to think about the primitive equipment we used. Our drums were a couple of electronic pads that tapped a beat along with the music. Our keyboard was a used Casio—and it sounded like it.

It's a cliché, but you get what you pay for. Over the years I have spent vast sums of money on quality equipment. One of the reasons the kids sound like pros is that they play the same equipment you would find in a studio.

I play a little bit of guitar, badly. I am even worse when it comes to keyboards and drums. Once again, I sought help at a music store. I sent a few students to learn how to do some basic drumming and paid for their lessons. These first drummers became the inspiration to a generation of percussionists. They in turn taught the next generation of Hobart Shakespeareans. I used a similar strategy with the piano. When I learned that a few kids in class had taken some lessons, I set up a system by which they taught other students.

I have also bought electronic drums for some of my students. These allow drummers to hear their work on headphones, which means they can bang away at home without driving their parents, and the neighbors, crazy. Electronic drums are expensive, but if you want good drummers in your class, the kids need to practice outside of school, too. We have an outstanding set of drums that we use for our Shakespeare productions, but the kids get good by practicing at home. On Saturdays, former student drummers help by teaching beginning percussionists at their apartments. I encourage my musicians to heed Gandalf's wise advice: "All you have to do is decide what to do with the time given you." More often than not, when the kids in Room 56 have spare time, they practice music.

It's like a snowball rolling downhill. The better the students sound, the easier it is to recruit eager new musicians. At this point, I am approached by third-graders who are interested in playing drums and want to start taking lessons from current students. I have only two requirements: One, they must take it seriously; and two, they have to learn to play one other instrument. I don't just want drummers—I want musicians. My current drummer, the best one I have ever encountered, is also a fine trombone player and guitarist. No wonder he plays with such passion.

In Concert

Playing in a band is great fun, and for many students the experience of playing music with their friends is motivation enough. But like the millions of starry-eyed young rockers who start bands to—how shall I say it?—*impress* the opposite sex, some of my students are also motivated by the opportunity it gives them to perform in front of audiences.

For instance, schools can use music at assemblies or other events to supplement the theme of the day. On Martin Luther King Jr. Day, schools often put on shows or skits to honor the man. A child may recite the "I have a dream" speech, or a class might hold up signs that display each letter of Dr. King's name and recite, "M is for Martin, he helped many people," and so forth. It's all fine, but it's so much finer to see a class belt out U2's "Pride." It's more engaging for the performers and for the audience. Whether an event is celebrating Independence Day, Veterans Day, Multicultural Day, or another holiday, it can always be made more exciting and poignant with a song.

One word of caution: If you ever plan to perform a song at an event off campus, please do a better job than I once did. Find out everything you can about the place where you will play. Many years ago, when our band was new, we were invited to sing a song for a large gathering of teachers. We loaded up our instruments and equipment and drove to an address I had written down on a scrap of paper. The students were psyched because we were unveiling our newest song, which featured a mandolin. I had taken a few lessons, and now one of my students, Susie, could play it well. We pulled up to the address, and the kids grew silent. We went in and played the song as best we could; the teachers liked it, but as we walked back to the van,

Susie told me we were all going to burn in hell. She might be right—I'm not sure a *church* was the place to perform REM's "Losing My Religion"!

Prisoner of Rock 'n' Roll

Once your class is rocking, you're lost forever. I don't drink, smoke, and or use any other drugs, but I'm addicted to rock and not close to recovery. If a good new song or a classic from the past finds its way to my ears, I can't simply listen and enjoy it. I'm always evaluating a song's potential for use with my students: Is the melody good enough that the kids won't tire of it during rehearsal? Is it musically interesting? Are there challenges within the song that will help my students become better musicians? And I'm always wondering if a song can be used in some larger context, which usually means our Shakespeare production that year or somewhere down the line.

It's why my wife will suddenly scare the hell out of me at 3:15 A.M. by grabbing me and urgently whispering, "Rafe, Clapton's 'Tears in Heaven'—you can use it for the child's funeral scene in *The Winter's Tale*!" Not to be outdone, I return the favor another night and wake her with the perfect song for Hamlet's opening soliloquy: "Paint It Black" by the Rolling Stones. There are so many terrific songs and not nearly enough time to rock with the class. But the kids never tire of it, and neither do I. The students in Room 56 play till their fingers bleed and their voices are gone. When I think about the amount of pressure kids are under today, combined with school environments that often resemble *Lord of the Flies,* I'm just grateful to have discovered a medium that allows my students to learn, have fun, and blow off steam at the same time.

How crazy is it to spend your life rocking with a group of young students? It's not only crazy, it's never ending. Recently, my class attempted the ultimate challenge in theater: *Hamlet*. As if spending a year learning and rehearsing an unabridged production of perhaps the world's greatest play weren't enough, the students added fourteen rock songs to the performance. And we're talking difficult pieces, such as Elton John's entire "Funeral for a Friend (Love Lies Bleeding)." The kids were harmonic perfection doing Paul Simon's "The Sound of Silence," sonically flawless on Radiohead's "Paranoid Android," and tragically epic when closing the shows with the Beatles' "While My Guitar Gently Weeps" (complete with Eric Clapton's blistering, unforgettable lead).

That should be enough to relax, right? Wrong. After a month of performances, my old student Joann took me out to dinner. She had flown in from Northwestern to watch the final show, and we laughed as we walked across the darkened parking lot she had crossed so many times as a little girl. We were short on time and went to a restaurant close to school. As we sat down at our table—before being served water, before evaluating the final performance of *Hamlet* and taking just a minute to breathe, reflect, and feel a little satisfaction at a truly extraordinary achievement by the children—Joann and I simultaneously asked each other, "So, what songs should we do for *Taming of the Shrew* next year?"

We laughed so hard we cried. We're addicted to the point of insanity. People in the restaurant looked at us like we were crazy, and they were right. We are crazy and proud of it. As Pete Townshend once remarked, "Rock 'n' roll might not solve your problems, but it does let you dance all over them."

SIXTEEN

Do They Know It's Christmas?

"See you the twenty-fourth." It's the standard good-bye I hear from former students who have stopped by to say hello from middle school, high school, or college. In Room 56, these few wonderful words sum up everything I want to teach my students. The words relate to an annual tradition of ours that tries to make the world a little better. The best way to help our children grow into exemplary people is often to involve them in projects that help other people.

Many schools offer community service programs. This is commendable, but most schools view community service as an assignment. Students pick up trash or remove graffiti and get a form signed to prove they completed their assignment. It's certainly better than not helping at all, but in Room 56 we do it a little differently. I want my students to reach Level VI. We help others because it's the right thing to do.

Every December 24, the Hobart Shakespeareans help feed, entertain, and clothe five hundred homeless people. Our Feed the World project teaches the kids to see the world outside their window and has inspired many of them to do community service on their own. I am reluctant to write about our program because it is contrary to the spirit of our class to talk about good deeds. All too often I see newspaper articles in which schools trumpet their community service. I think these schools miss an opportunity to teach their young people the sort of quiet humility that is part of Room 56. I would simply like to pass along an idea that I hope other teachers and parents might want to begin in their schools or add to the already good work they are doing.

The Phone Call

About twenty years ago, I received a phone call from a wonderful woman named Mimi Adams. She worked for an organization called Faith, which, among its many services, helps the homeless. They hosted an annual Christmas Eve lunch for the neighborhood's homeless people in a church basement. Mimi had heard I had a nice group of children and asked if the kids would come down and sing a few songs during the lunch. We accepted the invitation.

A few days later, about five of the kids came to the church with me. I brought a guitar, and the children sang three or four Christmas carols. After the kids finished their songs and started to leave the stage, the audience pleaded for more. When the kids explained that they didn't know any more songs, they were asked to sing the same songs again, which they did. I guess there's just something about the sound of children singing that manages to transport people out of their troubles.

I was amazed at the reaction of the children and the effect they had on the proceedings. It was a grim scene. For the students, it was the first time they had spent an extended amount of time with people they usually tried to avoid. They saw the effects of poverty, drug and alcohol abuse, and mental illness. They were also surprised to meet homeless people who were articulate, caring, and funny. The experience put a human face on the issue.

As we drove home that day, crammed in my little car, the kids started chattering about returning next Christmas. Before long, they had formulated a plan to return the following year with many more students and a lot more music.

Christmas Carols in April

These days my students rehearse Christmas songs all year long. Their repertoire has grown to include about fifty favorites, from classics like "Silent Night" to contemporary pop songs such as "Father Christmas" by the Kinks and "Happy Christmas (War Is Over)" by John Lennon and Yoko Ono. Their all-time favorite is "Do They Know It's Christmas?"—the 1984 Band Aid song that was played at the 1985 Live Aid concert heard and watched around the world. Each student receives a songbook with the lyrics to all the tunes we sing as well as copies of the songs on CDs.

The kids learn the songs over the course of the year. We usually spend about thirty minutes once a week practicing. It's easy because the students already know them from listening to their CDs. We simply arrange a few harmonies and choose different children to sing lead parts. It's always funny to see the quizzical looks we get from school visitors who pass our room and hear us singing "Jingle Bell Rock" in April.

These songs and the Feed the World project also provide an opportunity for the students to continue to develop as musicians. What began as a handful of students singing to my poorly strummed guitar has led to our class band learning all sorts of Christmas songs on guitars, keyboards, flutes, violins, and cellos. It's just one more way for these terrific musicians to hone their skills.

Several days before December 24, the homeless start to ask church workers, "Do you know if the kids are going to be here again?" Many of the homeless guys have told me the warmth of the children's voices and their beautiful smiles mean more to them than the food. The one problem we've encountered is that each year another thirty students are ready to sing, but the stage at the church is small. Since I didn't want to discourage former students from pitching in, we decided that anyone in seventh grade or above would help serve the food.

Preparation

On December 23, many of the former students who plan to serve food come to the church to set up the auditorium. In a matter of a few hours, tables and chairs are arranged. Decorations are put up everywhere. An auditorium that usually looks quite tired is transformed into a festive ballroom. All of the skills the students have learned in Room 56 come into play: They organize, work independently, show initiative, and function as a fabulous team. The kids divide up the labor. There is no squabbling about who will do what. A friend of mine who is the principal of an outstanding charter school once came to watch. He was interested in doing something similar with his students. His students have high test scores and their success has been deservedly acknowledged in the press, but as he watched dozens of young students independently and flawlessly set up a room for five hundred people, he shook his head. "This is what my students can't do," he said. "We're not there yet. I want them to be able to do *this*." Our Feed the World project may happen only once a year, but my students and I work every day to make it possible.

Clothing and Supplies

The kids save extra clothing and supplies throughout the year. Some parents help by collecting and buying socks. Others help prepare hy-

giene packets with soap, toothbrushes, toothpaste, and shampoo. It does not take a lot of time. The students simply put a few things away during the year, or buy a little something while they are shopping for themselves. By December 23, we have a huge collection of clothing and toiletries. These are organized by the students in two rooms in the church, one for women and one for men. The children set up racks and sort the clothing by size. On Christmas Eve, the homeless men and women find themselves in neat rooms stocked with useful clothing and supplies.

Former Students Pitch In

About a hundred current and former students help out on December 24. The fifth- and sixth-graders handle most of the singing and playing of instruments. Middle school students do most of the serving. To be frank, the kids in elementary school are too small to be serving food to the destitute. Most of the homeless people are terrific, but once in a while someone will get violent. Adults always step in when this happens, but I still feel better knowing my smallest students are up on the stage in safety. Middle school students are more adept at stepping out of such situations.

Eight homeless people sit at each table, and each table is served by two older students who spend their day running back and forth to the kitchen and making sure everyone at their table has everything he wants. While singing from the stage, the younger kids watch the scene and long to be down there amid the action. They always tell me they can't wait until they are older and can help serve the food, too.

The former students who return from high school and college work the rooms where people get clothing and supplies. It's difficult work. A terrific high school student named Rudy once came to me in frustration. One of the homeless men wanted a jacket, and Rudy showed him a rack with at least fifty good coats. The man told him, "Those aren't really my style. I need something in green." Rudy felt like telling the gentleman, "Hey, man, it is what it is. It's not like I can go and check our back stock!" We laughed, of course, but these frustrating moments are a good dose of reality for our young people. Working with the homeless increases the children's compassion and understanding for the less fortunate while also improving their poise, manners, and real-world knowledge. Parents and teachers who sponsor community service projects help the world and their own homes and classrooms—their kids become the kind of young people who are a pleasure to be around.

Higher and Higher

I want to emphasize that the Feed the World project was dreamed up by my students. It's the perfect example of what can happen when children are treated with respect and encouraged to live responsibly. They develop an awareness of the world around them that so many young people lack, and when they grow up, no matter what they do professionally, they continue to give back to their communities.

Former students who are now lawyers do pro bono work for the poor. Architects spend time on the side helping to design community centers or houses for Habitat for Humanity. One former student took a year off from college to work with poor children in Mongolia, and another spends two nights a week counseling troubled teens on a hotline. Still another former student, a young woman who received her master's in urban planning from MIT, has worked tirelessly to help the victims of Hurricane Katrina. These students are not Mother Teresa—they simply care about the world we live in and spend some time making it better.

I'm proud of my students for so many reasons. I love to celebrate with them when they are accepted to college, and four years later I love to attend their graduations and take pictures with them on that glorious day. But when all is said and done, I am most proud of their service to others. My favorite picture is one I received from Amy and Janet, two former students who were in India working with Habitat for Humanity. They stood in front of the Taj Mahal, smiling and holding a sign that read WE MISS YOU, RAFE. I get chills every time I look at it. They are the same chills I feel every time a former student signs off on an e-mail, hangs up the phone, or departs after a visit with the words "See you the twenty-fourth."

SEVENTEEN

Will Power

There is a reason the students in Room 56 are better known as the Hobart Shakespeareans. Each year, in addition to all the other projects and studies they undertake, the students produce and perform an unabridged play by Shakespeare. This requires the kids to work harder than they have ever worked in their lives as well as a teacher who is willing to sacrifice thousands of hours of personal time. More than a few observers, even those who admire the project and wish us well, have questioned my sanity and volunteered to get me some therapy. Perhaps they are right. All I know for sure is that I have found no other project that allows me to teach the students everything I want them to learn in a single activity.

Today the Hobart Shakespeareans are known around the world. People cross oceans to attend our performances. Sir Ian McKellen has been a guiding force behind the program, and Hal Holbrook, Michael York, Sir Peter Hall, and other giants of theater have helped inspire the students. Audience members often cannot believe what they are seeing. They watch ten-year-old kids perform flawless Shakespeare and ask, "How in the hell does all this happen?" Let me take you through a year in the life of a production, Hobart Shakespearean–style.

The Objectives

Before we do anything, I explain to the kids what I hope they will learn from the experience. They are not Shakespearean actors and probably should not plan to be. I know nothing about directing a play (if you don't believe me, come and watch a rehearsal—talk about the blind leading the blind!). We are here to learn about the power of language and to have fun working together as a team. The children will spend their year overcoming challenges, solving problems, and taking risks. They will learn a lot of difficult music and work hard to perform it well. They will learn to dance and to tell a story. They will explore themes in the play and apply these lessons to their own lives. They will analyze, dissect, tear down, and then build a play that will change their view of themselves and the world.

They are not here to impress anyone. The actual performances at the end of the year are fun—it's always nice to be on the receiving end of a standing ovation—but the real reward is in the work itself. No amount of applause can compare to the journey of discovery the kids undertake, the thousands of hours of work that go into making each production extraordinary. The process is all.

Choosing the Play

Most students are exposed to a very limited selection of Shakespeare. They might study *Hamlet, Julius Caesar, Romeo and Juliet, A Midsummer Night's Dream*, or *Macbeth*. These are great plays, and well worth reading or performing, but I want my kids to traverse the road less traveled. That's why the Hobart Shakespeareans have staged full productions of *Henry IV, Parts I and II; Twelfth Night; Measure for*

Measure; Love's Labour's Lost; The Comedy of Errors; King Lear; Much Ado About Nothing; The Winter's Tale; The Tempest; and *Henry V,* to name a handful. All of these plays contain themes of rich and profound relevance to the children.

Cynics who have never attended one of our shows sometimes doubt that the children really understand the words they are saying or the meaning behind them. They are dead wrong. The kids are engrossed by Prospero's resolution to forgive his enemies, Hal's search for honor in a dishonorable world, Isabella's heartbreaking decision to save her brother and forgo her own salvation, and Henry V's suffering for the sins of his father, to mention just a few examples. As Sir Ian McKellen has remarked, "The best thing about the Hobart Shakespeareans is that they know what they're saying, and that can't be said for all Shakespearean actors." I think it's a safe bet that Sir Ian knows what he's talking about.

I choose the plays a year or two before we put them on. This gives me plenty of time to study a play carefully and plan the rehearsals. There is no time to "find my way" with such an enormous undertaking. I need to be ready if I am to lead my students to the highest of highs.

Getting Started

The Hobart Shakespeareans meet and rehearse after school. We do this for two reasons. First, by asking students to volunteer for the activity, we weed out children who might not want to work as diligently as the rest of us. This is not a project for the disinterested. The production will consume a year of their lives. It means giving up things like television, video games, and pop-culture minutiae. It's serious business. Second, meeting after school allows students from other classes to join the fun. We are not an exclusive club. Anyone who is willing to be nice and work hard can participate.

There are a number of good books that summarize Shakespeare's plays. As a child, my mother read to me from the classic *Tales from Shakespeare* by Charles and Mary Lamb. I remember learning about *The Tempest* before I was in preschool. More recently, I have found my favorite summaries in Marchette Chute's *Stories from Shakespeare*. Unlike the Lamb volume, it summarizes *all* of the plays. The language is simple and direct.

I make copies of the summary, and we sit in class and read it together. By the end of our first meeting, the students understand the story we will be performing that year and the characters that drive it. They understand the play's themes and the objectives we will be trying to meet during our year together. The students leave the meeting eager to begin reading the actual play. There's only one problem: We never read Shakespeare.

Gently to Hear, Kindly to Judge, Our Play!

Shakespeare is a terrible read! His plays were never meant to be read. Michael York, the actor who played Tybalt in the 1968 film version of *Romeo and Juliet,* once reminded my students that in Shakespeare's day, people never said they were going to *see* a play but to *hear* one. The Bard can be flat-out confusing and boring when you read him— but nothing sounds better than hearing those miraculous words. When Patrick Stewart visited our class, he told the kids about his own childhood. He would listen to Shakespeare performances on the radio. He admitted that he didn't understand much of what he heard, but the words sounded so good he didn't care! He also told the children that despite all his success in television and film, the most exciting day of his life was when he was accepted as a member of the Royal Shakespeare Company.

Like Patrick Stewart and Michael York, the Hobart Shakespeareans learn the plays by listening. All of Shakespeare's plays are available on CD through a company called Arkangel. You can buy the plays individually or as a complete boxed set. These CDs are invaluable to my students. By hearing professional actors speak the words, the kids get a far-reaching understanding of whatever play we're listening to.

As with all audio lessons, I stop the CD at certain points to explain particular phrases. I let some expressions pass at first. After hearing a scene several more times, the students catch on. It is amazing how quickly the kids can learn lines when they understand the words. It's no different from the pop songs they learn from the radio.

Which Text?

There are enough Shakespeare publishers to make one's head spin. I suppose every teacher has his favorite. We've had good success with Folger editions, which are inexpensive and offer brief summaries before every scene. This reminds the students what is about to take place. The Folger editions also feature notes that run throughout the text, a setup that allows the reader to make sense of puzzling passages without flipping to the back of the book.

Some new editions of Shakespeare print the actual text of the play on the left page and modern translations of the meaning on the right page. I can understand why this would be attractive to some teachers; it makes the text more accessible to beginners. But I worry that it would be *too* accessible—students might not read Shakespeare's words at all. One of our objectives is to mine the text for hidden jewels. We are not looking for a shortcut. I want the students to struggle a bit, overcome the language barriers, and make exciting discoveries about the power of Shakespeare's words. By studying the actual text, students are also more likely to find the Shakespearean rhythm when they begin speaking their lines.

Will on Film

All of Shakespeare's plays are available as movies—in the 1980s, the BBC filmed every play he wrote—and most are available in a number of different versions. Naturally, some adaptations are better than others. No matter how good or bad the film is, I always find it effective to watch a scene immediately after reading it. There's no accounting for taste, but here are a few of my favorite Shakespeare films to supplement the study of the plays:

Macbeth	There are several good versions of this play. I would try the Royal Shakespeare Company production with Sir Ian McKellen and Dame Judi Dench. It really shows the kids how a small space can be used in a play. Roman Polanski's film is incredibly bloody, but very well done.
Henry V	I love to let the kids compare Sir Laurence Olivier's unabashedly patriotic adaptation to Kenneth Branagh's post-Vietnam tragedy.
Richard III	Olivier's version is diabolically funny and also stars Sir John Gielgud and Sir Ralph Richardson. Ian McKellen's version is just as brilliant and offers a very creative take on the story.
Twelfth Night	Trevor Nunn made a fine film a few years ago that stars Sir Ben Kingsley as Feste the Fool.
A Midsummer Night's Dream	If you want your kids to hear Shakespeare's words as they were meant to be spoken, Sir Peter Hall's 1968 film is a must. Diana Rigg, Judi Dench, Helen Mirren, and Ian Holm have a muddy ball in this all-star romp.

Even a bad film can help students prepare to perform Shakespeare. My students recently watched the BBC version of *Love's La-*

bour's Lost, which they did not like at all. Yet examining why they took issue with several performances brought the young actors closer to where they wanted to go with the characters.

Speaking Shakespeare

Many visitors to our class wonder how the kids memorize so many lines. What most observers don't understand is that the real difficulty lies in comprehending the words, not in memorizing them. I take the time to go over every syllable of every word with the students. As we listen to the CD of a play, we pause and break down the language. It's a heck of a lot easier for the kids to memorize words they understand. Next, I burn CDs of the scenes for all the actors, who listen to them at home. Shakespeare is just like music. Instead of memorizing thousands of lines of pop music, the Hobart Shakespeareans use the same energy to memorize beautiful language. It is astonishing how quickly children learn by listening. There is only one drawback to this strategy. The plays are performed by British actors, and every year a few of my students start speaking with British accents. We all laugh and encourage each other to speak in our own voices. We're not here to be Olivier or McKellen. It's just a bunch of little kids having fun.

We play two games in the classroom to help the kids become comfortable speaking out loud. The first is as simple as it sounds: Thirty-seven Plays. The kids take turns calling out the titles of all the plays Shakespeare wrote, and each title can be said only once. We often begin a rehearsal this way. As the kids shout out *Hamlet, Henry V,* and *The Comedy of Errors,* they have to listen to one another so that titles are not repeated. It's quite funny early in the year when they make mistakes. I once had to explain to a student that, though I admired the passion with which his answer was delivered, *Green Eggs and Ham* was not, in fact, written by Shakespeare.

The second exercise grew out of an ingenious short essay, "On Quoting Shakespeare," by the late English journalist Bernard Levin. A Google search will lead you to this clever piece of prose, which is a delightful reminder of how many Shakespearean expressions we use daily without realizing it. When something has "vanished into thin air" or you have had "too much of a good thing" or didn't "sleep a wink," you have been quoting Shakespeare. If you've ever "refused to budge an inch" or "played fast and loose" or even "knitted your brows," you've been quoting Shakespeare. The kids fire off the quotes in rapid succession. This is also a terrific way to begin or end a rehearsal.

Casting the Plays

In our year-round school, classes begin in July. We spend at least a month learning the play we will be performing the following April. After meeting four times a week for an hour, the students know the play well. They have listened to the entire play and have watched various film adaptations. If I open the play and read even the most obscure of lines, the students will be able to identify the speaker.

Casting the play is easy; casting it *well* is not. Around the middle of August, I give the kids a sheet of paper and ask them to list a few roles they would like to play in order of preference. Note that students are not required to try out for speaking roles. Some want to be in the band. Others want to be a part of the technical crew. Most of the children do more than one job, and that's fine. Part of the beauty of producing a play is that there is something challenging for each child to do.

Next we have tryouts, which show me who is best suited for each role. But good acting, like most endeavors, is ten percent inspiration and ninety percent perspiration. At this point in the year, I have known the students for only about a month, and it's almost impossible to predict which of them will put in the vigorous effort it takes to play a leading role well. I work with about sixty students after school, and many of them are not even in my class during the day.

As a result, the tentative cast list I prepare in August usually changes a number of times before the play is actually performed eight months later. There will probably be students who do not meet the standard you have set. However, there are always young people who rise to levels you couldn't have imagined when you first met them. Many years ago, I cast a student named Larry to play Caliban in *The Tempest*. For months I worked with Larry and encouraged him to do his best. His initial reading of the part won him the role, but his work ethic was somewhere between comatose and DOA. I didn't want to give up on Larry, but the play was drawing nearer and the other students were fantastic. One day Larry had to miss part of a rehearsal. A student named Danny, who had spent the previous six months singing a little and watching a lot, was asked to fill in. His acting was sensational! He knew the entire part and walked onstage as though he had played Caliban for years.

This is a common occurrence, so I am flexible with casting. After a few months of rehearsal, all of the students know the play by heart anyway. The kids must learn to set aside their egos. They are taught that there is only one star in the production: Shakespeare himself.

There's No Place Like Home

Our Shakespeare productions are performed right in our classroom. We clear the room of desks and install a bleacher section that seats thirty-three. The actual performance space is perhaps two hundred square feet. Despite the tiny area, we are able to perform unabridged plays complete with sensational choreography, a full-blown rock 'n' roll band, and perfectly articulated Shakespeare.

There are no sets or costumes. Those things take too much time, and while they look pretty, they have nothing to do with our mission. The students wear only jeans and our Hobart Shakespearean T-shirts. The shirts are different colors, and those colors are the only hint of costumes in the show. Royalty normally wears purple. The band wears turquoise. Rebels wear red, and jealous husbands wear green. It works beautifully. By forgoing sets and costumes, we make sure Shakespeare's language is the star of the play. The audience, sitting not four feet from the actors, experiences a play like never before. People who have watched Shakespeare for years have remarked that our productions had them listening to the words more carefully than they ever had in their lives.

Of course, this intimacy can have its drawbacks. Many years ago the children were putting on *Macbeth*, and a lovely teacher I know brought her father, who was in the early stages of Alzheimer's disease. When Macbeth went into his tense "Is this a dagger I see before me?" speech, he pulled out the stage knife he would use to kill King Duncan. Upon seeing the knife, this poor old man began yelling, "Ooooo! He's got a knife! He's got a knife! He's going to *kill* someone!" I'm not sure what was funnier—the audience trying to hush the poor guy, or watching the boy who was playing Macbeth think about using the knife on someone other than the king!

But seriously, there's no place like home. Even though my students are invited to perform on huge stages in front of massive audiences, we've learned that it's more memorable and educational to stage plays right in the classroom. After all, these productions aren't about the amount of applause or the length of standing ovations—they're about language, music, teamwork, risk, discipline, hard work, and self-discovery. And by performing the plays right in our classroom, we're much closer to what Shakespeare did in his own day.

Using Music and Dance

Many years ago, the Hobart Shakespeareans were performing *A Midsummer Night's Dream*. These were the early days of our productions, which were terrific but nothing like the shows we put on today. Still, the basic minimalist structure of the show was in place, and the students were learning a lot. When we arrived at the scene in which Titania goes to sleep and asks her fairies for a song, we inserted a pop song rather than the tune Shakespeare had used. I felt the scene needed a little extra push. It must have, because during one of the shows the little girl playing Titania actually fell asleep on the stage. Ah, these method actors!

The song was the highlight of the show. It was only a simple tune, with the kids singing and me playing a little guitar in the background (I was so blind in those days). The fairies did a modest dance, based on choreography I badly copied from several different numbers I had seen in various films. Despite the lack of vision on my part, the scene worked very well. By the following year, the Hobart Shakespeareans had become a very different force.

These days, people describe our shows as rock concerts disguised as Shakespeare. The text of the play is never altered, but we throw in a dozen or more songs to spice things up. During the first two months of rehearsals, the students learn to play and sing dozens of potential tunes that might enhance a particular scene in the play. By the third month of rehearsals, our song list is in place. For the next six months, the band rehearses constantly and the singers diligently work out the vocals. Soon the show's sound track is ready.

The coolest part of all this is that the songs are interwoven with the text. When a character has a soliloquy, or a regular scene allows it, the song begins, then stops while the scene continues, then starts again, and so on. It's almost like opera. We've used John Lennon's "Jealous Guy" when Leontes begs forgiveness in *The Winter's Tale*; the Animals' "Please Don't Let Me Be Misunderstood" as Henry V prays before battle; the Temptations' "Ain't Too Proud to Beg" when Master Ford asks his wife to take him back in *The Merry Wives of Windsor*; and REM's "Everybody Hurts" layered over Hamlet's "To be, or not to be." All of the songs are played and sung with precise attention to detail. To add to the experience, my friend Barbara Hayden teaches many of the students sign language. By having some of the performers sign the songs, another layer of communication is added to the show. It's very powerful.

The students also perform two or three spectacular dance numbers during each play. The dances are choreographed by a number of terrific local instructors, all accomplished modern dancers in their own right. I know these kids are not Shakespearean actors, and the dance instructors know they are not professional dancers (though they are after a year of lessons!). But we all know the value of bringing together different artistic mediums to produce a fabulous show and teach the kids as much as possible. In *The Taming of the Shrew*, for example, the students treated the Katherine character to a hilarious satirical dance that was set to Dusty Springfield's "Wishin' and Hopin'," and the Bianca character was the object of a sultry dance set to OK Go's "You're So Damn Hot." We are currently working on a terrifying piece for the witches in *Macbeth* that will be danced as the band blasts the Rolling Stones' "Sympathy for the Devil."

Speaking Shakespeare's words, playing great songs, and dancing through it all is a killer combination. The kids have so much fun rehearsing, they hardly realize how much they're learning.

Intermission

When I was a beginning teacher, I used to travel around to different arts programs and look for ideas. One night I stopped by a prestigious private school to watch a play. It was pretty good. These were rich kids, and many of them had been taught by private drama coaches. A lot of money was up on the stage. There were also fancy lights, special effects, and carefully designed moments to impress the crowd. Then came intermission. It was a hot spring night, and the large crowd fought through the rear of the auditorium to get some air. In the lobby I encountered a few folding tables that held paper plates, half-empty boxes of stale graham crackers, and warm bottles of soda. Paper cups were scattered about in such a way that I couldn't tell which cups had been used and which hadn't. I vowed to learn from this. I decided to use intermission itself as a learning device.

Our productions usually run for three weeks. Each show is about three hours long. An hour before the show, the students go into the room adjacent to ours. They set up tables, scrub them, and cover them with elegant tablecloths. Parents arrive with gorgeous flower displays. These same parents arrive with a vast selection of fresh fruit, vegetables, and appetizers, along with a variety of cold and hot drinks. I provide the funds, and the parents donate the most valuable thing of all—their time.

During intermission, the Shakespeareans serve the audience members. The people in the audience are our guests, and we want them to feel welcome and appreciated. The actors listen to the audience, engage in conversation, and behave like the kind of young people who make adults believe the future might be okay after all.

When the show ends and the applause fades, the actors go back next door and clean the room. Hamlet and Ophelia may have just received a standing ovation, but five minutes later they're right there scrubbing the floor and moving tables with everyone else. The students understand that this part of the evening says just as much about who they are as the three hours that preceded it.

Wait Till Next Year

Outside the Elizabethan Stage in Ashland, the Oregon Shakespeare Festival hangs a shield for each play that has been performed there since 1935. We've borrowed this good idea and hang shields in our room as well.

Each year we perform a ritual during the final bow. As the lead performers walk offstage, the youngest students stay behind. These are fourth-graders who were not in Room 56 during the daily lessons but joined the production after school. As the stage clears, these little ones reach behind a large picture of Shakespeare that has stared at the crowd from the front of the room. They pull out the newest shield, which announces next year's production in large letters. The fourth-graders wave good night and shout, "See you next year," and the audience is already making plans to return. The king is dead. Long live the king. The Hobart Shakespeareans begin the next year's show before the current one is even finished.

It's symbolic of Room 56's never-ending cycle of work, play, and excellence. There is no finish line. The show is astonishing, but it's just another day in the life for these children. It's a part of who they are, and the lessons of Shakespeare are forever stamped on their souls. Never was this more evident than when a PBS crew recently asked a student to name his favorite book. He answered with *The Adventures of Huckleberry Finn*. When asked why, the boy responded, "Mark

Twain held the mirror up to nature." Without blinking an eye, this student was using Hamlet to express his own beliefs and thoughts. I guess the poet and dramatist Ben Jonson was right: Shakespeare was not of an age, but for all time.

Rest in Peace

It's a thankless job. It's hard to find a reason to believe.

It's thankless and it doesn't get easier. When you glance at your mental ledger, the red ink completely dominates the black. For every reason to believe, for every child you may help, there are dozens who make you want to give up. Most of the kids who walk into our classrooms do not even begin to comprehend how education can help them improve their lives. They often come from families so poor or scared or mean that you cannot even go to them for help.

Many of your administrators have sold their souls years before. Do you have a dangerous child in your class? Will you get any backup to deal with the problem? Most often you won't. The lawyers have seen to that, frightening school districts so that no one takes a stand anymore. In fact, when the child threatens someone's life, *you* may be blamed for running the sort of classroom where that sort of thing could happen.

The "Ministry of Truth" continues to spread its lies. The publishing companies and testing services conspire with the administrators to wrest away any creativity, passion, or freedom you once may have had as a classroom teacher. From now on we will all teach the same things in the same ways at the same times for the same reasons. Orwell the Prophet was right.

So you continue to look for a reason to believe, and your search brings you to your students. At least they might be able to give you comfort. But so many do not. For every child who is ready and willing to make the effort, far more have given up because of the same forces that make *us* want to surrender.

Maybe the realists are right. Maybe it is quixotic to want an excellent education for our students. There are days (and nights) when I come dangerously close to surrender. When I toss and turn thinking of all my failures, I open Janet's essay. It is an essay she wrote at Notre Dame. I took her there when she was thirteen years old. I told her it was possible. She is a top student there today. My search for a reason to believe ends here.

My heart begins to beat as the lights start to dim and the chattering of students slowly dies down from scattered mumblings to silence. The tiny room is flooded with lights, and I look out into the audience. An eleven-year-old boy walks out onto the stage, or classroom, I should say, to speak the opening lines of his character, Benedict.

My heart starts to beat again quite rapidly as my turn approaches. The crowd laughs and I take it as my cue to step onto the stage. "I wonder that you will still be talking, Signior Benedict: nobody marks you." It is 6:00 P.M. on June 15, 1998, and I have just started my twelfth and final performance of Shakespeare's *Much Ado About Nothing*.

I was first introduced to Shakespeare when I was nine years old by a teacher, Rafe Esquith, who was famously known at my elementary school for directing a Shakespeare play every year. Not wanting to turn down an opportunity to be in one of his "famous" plays, I immediately said yes when he asked me.

Now I put "famous" in quotes because, at my elementary school, being asked to participate in a Shakespeare play was like being asked to join the cool and exclusive group in school.

The following year I was given the opportunity to be in *The Winter's Tale*. All the plays were performed in our tiny classroom, Room 56, and on that night of the final performance I could only think to wish that I could stop time.

I wish I could put all the feelings from that evening into a jar and carry it around with me wherever I go, because the emotions in Room 56 that night were full of delight, passion, and energy. Putting together those plays every year not only taught me about Shakespeare, but about teamwork, and humility, and that when one of my fellow classmates was on stage, it was his turn to be in the spotlight, not mine.

I learned how to play many instruments because we incorporated pop songs into many of the scenes. I learned the value of responsibility and hard work, that if I did not have my lines memorized by a specific date, it not only hurt myself, but slowed down the rest of the production.

Who would have thought that one could learn so much just by being in a play? I learned my most valuable lessons during those two years in Room 56, and I treasure all of my experiences that I had in that tiny little classroom.

Hobart Elementary School is located in the heart of downtown L.A., and as I look back at my elementary school years, I think about the horrible environment I grew up in.

There were kids who didn't know how to speak English,

even teachers who did not know how to speak English. A rape or abuse case occurred at least once a week at school, and policemen were frequently seen on campus.

Yet during the fifth grade, when I walked into Room 56, everything changed. The world outside disappeared. Instead of gang fights and beggars, my life turned into guitar lessons, road trips, and Shakespearean characters.

My fears and horrors were replaced by happiness and laughter. It became my second home, and my classmates became my second family. I did most of my growing up in Room 56, and it molded me into the person I have become.

No matter what else was happening anywhere in the world, all my troubles could be fixed in this safe haven, and I constantly retreated to it when I had family troubles. And even today, when I am looking for a place where there is only love and joy, where anger and hatred do not exist, I still retreat to Room 56.

As usual, it is a student who proves to be my best teacher. There *is* a reason to believe. Let us all work hard to build these safe havens. Janet's essay eases my sleep. Tomorrow, as always, I, too, will retreat to Room 56. There's no place like home.

Acknowledgments

Room 56 is one of those cosmic miracles where the whole is bigger than the sum of its parts. Like the Beatles, the Brooklyn Dodgers, and *Casablanca*, the magic is the result of timing, talent, and luck. Patrons, celebrities, other teachers, and my wife, Barbara, have all played major roles in creating this unique haven.

My agent, Bonnie Solow; my publisher, Clare Ferraro; my editors, Jofie Ferrari-Adler and Wendy Wolf, and all my friends at Viking Penguin have provided extraordinary support for this book.

But the key players to be recognized are the children. Every child in Room 56 has displayed courage, perseverance, and a passion that many of their peers lack. These are children who bravely walk roads less traveled. They are kind when their world is mean and work incredibly hard when others give up. These kids do not make excuses. They seize opportunities and give all who meet them hope for the future.

Hobart Shakespeareans, thank you for inspiring teachers like me to try harder. Thank you for your guidance, your brilliance, and your laughter. No book can capture the tactile joy that everyone feels when they enter the room you created. I am so lucky to be a small part of it.

APPENDIX A

Hooray for Hollywood

By watching films at home on weekends, after school on Tuesdays, and as part of our curriculum, each student in Room 56 will watch over one hundred films during the school year. Here are twenty-five films that every student experiences. These films help the students connect and relate to the history, literature, and values that are part of being a Hobart Shakespearean.

1. *The African Queen*
2. *The Best Years of Our Lives*
3. *Casablanca*
4. *Charade*
5. *E.T.*
6. *Glory*
7. *A Hard Day's Night*
8. *High Noon*
9. *In the Heat of the Night*
10. *Inherit the Wind*
11. *It's a Wonderful Life*
12. *Malcolm X*
13. *Miracle on 34th Street*
14. *Mr. Smith Goes to Washington*
15. *Modern Times*
16. *On the Waterfront*
17. *Saving Private Ryan*
18. *Schindler's List*
19. *Some Like It Hot*
20. *Star Wars*
21. *The Sting*
22. *To Kill a Mockingbird*
23. *Twelve Angry Men*
24. *West Side Story*
25. *The Wizard of Oz*

Sample Washington, D.C., Itinerary

As the Hobart Shakespeareans plan trips with a "Less is more" philosophy, there are dozens of worthwhile activities missing from this schedule. This is just to give you ideas as you arrange your own itinerary. Weather, time, and areas of class interest will guide you in planning the perfect trip for your students. For example, we do not visit the Holocaust Museum because we have the similar Museum of Tolerance in Los Angeles.

Dinners are usually at 4:30 at restaurants near our final stop or back at the hotel. After reading, the kids are normally in bed by 8:30.

Saturday		We fly from Los Angeles to Washington, D.C. We fly on Saturday because the Metro system is less crowded when we arrive, making it easy for us to get from Reagan National Airport to our hotel.
Sunday	Morning	Arlington National Cemetery Marine Corps Memorial
	Afternoon	Lunch is often at Union Station near our hotel. This is the lightest day of the trip. The children are often tired because of jet lag. We are back at the hotel by 3:00.
Monday	Morning	Washington Monument (advance tickets available online) World War II Memorial

	Afternoon	Lunch at Smithsonian National Museum of American History, before tour of selected exhibits
Tuesday	Morning	Line up for 9:00 tour of Ford's Theatre (We call the day before to ensure tours are running.) Peterson House (where Lincoln died)
	Afternoon	Lunch at National Gallery of Art Tour of selected exhibits in west and east wings
Wednesday	Morning	Tour of White House (tickets arranged through congressperson months in advance)
	Afternoon	Lunch at Smithsonian National Museum of Natural History before tour of selected exhibits
Thursday	Morning	Mount Vernon (tour through Gray Line or Tourmobile) and lunch there
	Afternoon	Return at 2:00 to hotel for afternoon nap
	Evening	Attend performance at Shakespeare Theater
Friday	Morning	Supreme Court U.S. Capitol (tour arranged through congressperson's office) Folger Shakespeare Library
	Afternoon	Lunch at Smithsonian National Air and Space Museum and tour of exhibits
Saturday	Morning	Pack sack lunches for our walking tour: Albert Einstein Memorial Vietnam Veterans Memorial Korean War Veterans Memorial Lincoln Memorial

	Lunch	Picnic on the Mall
	Afternoon	FDR Memorial The Jefferson Memorial
	Evening	Pack for return tomorrow
Sunday	Morning	Return to Los Angeles. If we take an early-morning flight, we keep in mind that the Metro has reduced hours on Sundays.

NOTE: We often eat lunch at Union Station, near the Capitol, where there are a number of inexpensive choices. Another excellent place to eat is the food court in the Ronald Reagan Building at Federal Triangle. Adults will need to show picutre I.D.s to enter the building.

APPENDIX C

Rock 'n' Roll Shakespeare

Hobart Shakespearean productions are a unique blend of text and music. A live band rocks, singers belt out tunes, and dancers fly across the tiny stage to help tell the story. Here are some examples of plays we have performed, along with the music we have incorporated into them. We've gotten better and far more elaborate over the years.

The Tempest
1994

"Venus and Mars" (Paul McCartney)	The play opens with Prospero studying his magic.
Suite in E Minor (J. S. Bach)	This plays as Prospero tells his daughter, Miranda, her life story.
"Are You Sitting Comfortably?" (The Moody Blues)	Miranda helps Ferdinand carry wood after her father assigns him difficult duties.
"Dream On" (Aerosmith)	Prospero creates a magic play for the islanders.
"Grow Old with Me" (John Lennon)	Miranda and Ferdinand get married.

"The Heart of the Matter" (Don Henley)	The kids bow during this song of forgiveness.

The Merchant of Venice
1995

"Right Now" (Van Halen)	The play opens linking the prejudice against Shylock with hatred in the world today.
"I Still Haven't Found What I'm Looking For" (U2)	The merchant Antonio tells his troubles to the audience and his young friend Bassanio.
Suite in C Major for Four Guitars (Paul Peuerl)	This classical piece is used every time the scene shifts to the romantic setting of Belmont.
"Love Will Keep Us Alive" (The Eagles)	Shylock's daughter, Jessica, is persuaded to elope with Lorenzo.
"Sympathy for the Devil" (The Rolling Stones)	Shylock plots his revenge against Antonio.
"One" (U2)	Jessica ponders her unhappiness as she enters the Christian world and sadly dances at a party.
"Losing My Religion" (REM)	We close the show and bow to this rocker.

Hamlet
2004

"Funeral for a Friend (Love Lies Bleeding)" (Elton John)	King Hamlet's funeral opens the play, accompanied by this song.

"Paint It Black" This is played during Hamlet's soliloquy on the
(The Rolling Stones) weariness he feels with the world.

"Dreams of Our Fathers" The Ghost visits Hamlet.
(Dave Matthews)

"Lithium" Hamlet begins to go mad. He plans to put on
(Nirvana) a play.

"Lonesome Day" This opens the action after our first intermission.
(Bruce Springsteen)

"Everybody Hurts" With sign language included, this is played during
(REM) Hamlet's "To be, or not to be" speech.

"Reason to Believe" Hamlet is crushed by Ophelia.
(Rod Stewart)

"Paranoid Android" Claudius prays while Hamlet considers murdering
(Radiohead) him.

"I'll Feel a Whole Hamlet switches letters and plots the death of
Lot Better" Rosencrantz and Guildenstern.
(The Byrds)

"Ruby Tuesday" Ophelia loses her mind.
(The Rolling Stones)

"Out of Time" Ophelia commits suicide.
(The Rolling Stones)

"The Sound of Silence" Ophelia is buried as Hamlet watches.
(Paul Simon)

"Lost Cause" Hamlet prepares for his duel with Laertes.
(Beck)

"While My Guitar George Harrison's solo acoustic version plays as
Gently Weeps" Hamlet dies, and the classic rock arrangement
(The Beatles) accompanies the final bows.

The Taming of the Shrew
2005

Concerto in D Major (Vivaldi)	Four classical guitars and two keyboards play this music to link scenes together.
"Refugee" (Tom Petty)	This opens the play, to set up Kate's treatment by her family.
"You're So Damn Hot" (OK Go)	The men of Padua worship Bianca as this dance sequence introduces her to the play.
"I'm Not Like Everybody Else" (The Kinks)	This is performed during the first meeting of Kate and Petruchio.
"Substitute" (The Who)	Hortensio, Tranio, and Lucentio all disguise themselves.
"Tired of Waiting for You" (The Kinks)	Kate is left standing at the altar when Petruchio is late.
"We Can Work It Out" (The Beatles)	Kate decides to leave her home and follow Petruchio after her disastrous wedding.
"Such Great Heights" (The Postal Service)	This opens the show after intermission.
"Under My Thumb" (The Rolling Stones)	Petruchio tames Kate by withholding food and sleep.
"Wishin' and Hopin'" (Dusty Springfield)	Kate has a dream in which angels teach her how to please her husband. A hilarious dance accompanies the song.
"Maybe I'm Amazed" (Paul McCartney)	Kate helps her husband win the bet to conclude the play.

| "I Feel Fine" (The Beatles) | With its unforgettable lead guitar (with feedback!), this song accompanies the final bows. |

Love's Labour's Lost
2006

Concerto in D Major (Vivaldi)	Four guitars play the entire concerto, with different movements opening the show at Part II after intermission.
"I Am a Rock" (Paul Simon)	King Ferdinand writes his proclamation for Navarre.
"Boulevard of Broken Dreams" (Green Day)	The proclamation is read to Navarre and the king's friends sign the oath.
"The Village Green Preservation Society" (The Kinks)	The Queen of France and her court arrive in Navarre to encounter the new rules. The students present the lyrics in sign language.
"I Can't Explain" (The Who)	The men break the rules and fall in love with the women.
"The One I Love" (REM)	The men write secret love letters to the women.
"Vertigo" (U2)	The men and women dance dizzily and fall in love.
"Ticket to Ride" (The Beatles)	As Part II begins, the women are more than willing to leave the men and their kingdom.
"Wonderwall" (Oasis)	The men plan to send their ladies presents to win their love.
"Back in the USSR" (The Beatles)	The men dress up as Russians and dance to entertain their women.

"Fix You"
(Coldplay)

The Princess of France receives word of her father's death.

"Patience"
(Guns N' Roses)

The men will have a year to prove themselves worthy of the ladies.

"Days"
(The Kinks)

The kids' final bows are accompanied by this classic.

Macbeth
2007

"Riders on the Storm"
(The Doors)

The witches enter to this classic, complete with Ray Manzarek's entire piano solo.

"Beware of Darkness"
(George Harrison)

Banquo warns Macbeth about temptation. The verses weave in and out of their conversation, and sign language completes the scene.

"Here We Go"
(Jon Brion)

Lady Macbeth reads Macbeth's letter and chooses her course of action.

"A Town Called Malice"
(The Jam)

King Duncan and his people dance wildly at Macbeth's castle to celebrate their victory in the war.

"For Your Love"
(The Yardbirds)

Macbeth is convinced by his wife to kill King Duncan while the party continues. Dancers freeze in the background between verses as the Macbeths plot the murder.

"How to Disappear Completely"
(Radiohead)

King Duncan is murdered.

"I'm So Tired"
(The Beatles)

Macbeth complains to his wife that his mind is "full of scorpions." He hints at his plan to murder Banquo.

"Come As You Are"   Banquo is murdered in the forest as his son
(Nirvana)   escapes. The death concludes Part I.

"Scarborough Fair" /   Part II opens with four students singing this
"Canticle"   classic, complete with harpsichord, Ovation guitar,
(Simon and Garfunkel)   and four-part harmony.

"Sympathy for the Devil"   The witches dance menacingly and prepare for
(The Rolling Stones)   Macbeth's arrival.

"No Suprises"   Lady Macduff is murdered, and the song
(Radiohead)   bridges into the following scene where Macduff
                            hears the horrible news.

"Trouble"   Lady Macbeth sleepwalks and reveals her
(Cat Stevens)   tortured mind.

"Sixty Years On"   In candlelight, Macbeth hears about his wife's
(Elton John)   death, and recites the famous "tomorrow, and
                            tomorrow, and tomorrow" speech.

"Sunday Bloody Sunday"   The cast bows during this classic rocker, and
(U2)   reveals *As You Like It* as the 2008 offering.

A Day in the Life

6:30 A.M.	Doors to Room 56 open. Students have the option to come early. Kids work on projects, music, and cleaning the room.
7:00 A.M.	Math team (optional) Kids work on problem solving.
8:00 A.M.	School officially begins. Grammar exercises
8:30 A.M.	Math
9:30 A.M.	Literature
10:30 A.M.	U.S. History
11:00 A.M.	Recess Optional classical guitar lessons for interested students
11:20 A.M.	Science
12:00 P.M.	Geography or Economics
12:30 P.M.	Lunch Optional rock guitar lessons for interested students
1:20 P.M.	Fine Arts
2:20 P.M.	Physical Education
3:00 P.M.	Traditional school day ends. Shakespeare begins.
4:30 P.M.	Shakespeare ends. Students go home or stay in the room to study or clean.
6:00 P.M.	Most students have left for home. Some stay to continue their studies.

Seven Ways Parents Can Help Their Children Beyond or Outside the Classroom

1. A lot of kids today can't do all the things we learned in Home Ec or Shop. Those kinds of classes are disappearing. Teach your child to cook lasagna, sew on a button, plant a seedling, or change a tire. If your child has these simple, useful skills and others like them, he or she will be on the road to self sufficiency and far more likely to do well in college, when real life begins.

2. Elementary parents need to spend time in the classroom, every month if possible. Your kids will hate it when they're teens, but little kids really love it when a parent shows up and participates, even if it's only for an hour or two. Bringing in home cooked brownies for a party or the school play will make your child's day.

3. Have a family movie night once a week (on a nonschool night). If possible, pick classic films that are connected either with times of the year or subjects being studied in school. Help your child understand that learning is a full-time job and does not end at 3:00.

4. iPODs are great (nobody loves music more than me!), but not in public. Children should be opening their eyes and ears to the world around them, not shutting it out.

5. Help your child stay away from screens, too. They are everywhere—gas stations, airports, bathrooms, supermarket lines, ball games, public buses. It's something right out of *Fahrenheit 451*. Kids need to be watching less and doing more when they're out in the world. And parents need to set an example here—don't catch yourself staring at CNN while waiting for the table at a restaurant. And no television on a school night—ever—for you or them. There are better things to do.

6. Make sure your children take part in dinner, and that includes the preparation and clean up afterward, not just sitting down together to eat. And remember—this should definitely not be in front of a TV screen. How can you talk if you're all starting at yet another screen?

7. Holidays are great opportunities for more than overeating and football. Children today have no idea of why they have certain days like Veterans Day or Presidents Day off from school. Each holiday, from Labor Day to Memorial Day, is an opportunity for parents to teach their kid history, tradition, and help connect the child to our nation. Through watching an appropriate movie, reading a book or story together, or visiting a military cemetery and placing flowers on graves on November 11, children become more aware of how they're a part of history, and they'll be taking a big step toward being better citizens.